C000127523

art

Moving Millions
A Pictorial History of London Transport

Best wishes
Graham Miller

Moving Millions

A PICTORIAL HISTORY OF LONDON TRANSPORT

THEO BARKER

London Transport
Museum

MOVING MILLIONS:
A Pictorial History of London Transport
by Theo Barker.

Published jointly by
London Transport Museum
Covent Garden
London
WC2E 7BB
and
Book Production Consultants
47 Norfolk Street
Cambridge CB1 2LE.

Published 1990.

© London Transport Museum and Book
Production Consultants, 1990.

British Library Cataloguing in Publication Data
Barker, T. C. Theodore Cardwell *1923–*
Moving millions: a pictorial history of
London transport.
1. London. Public transport services: London
Transport, history
I. Title
388.4065421

ISBN 1-871829-03-8
ISBN 1-871829-02-X pbk

All rights reserved. No part of this publication
may be reproduced, stored in a retrieval system
or transmitted in any form or by any means,
electronic, mechanical, photocopying,
recording or otherwise, without the prior
permission of the publishers.

Design and production by
Book Production Consultants.

Designed by Peter Dolton.

Index compiled by Jean Macqueen.

Typeset by Anglia Photoset, Colchester.

Printed and bound in the United Kingdom by
BPCC Hazell Books Ltd, Aylesbury HP20 1LB.

The opinions expressed in this book are the author's and do not necessarily represent the views of either London Transport or the London Transport Museum.

The book attempts to bring out the main points in *A History of London Transport*, a two-volume work written some years ago in collaboration with Michael Robbins, who spent all his working life in London Transport, retiring in 1978 as Managing Director (Railways). A much-respected transport man – he served as President of the Chartered Institute of Transport in 1975–76 – his spare-time preoccupation has always been the history of the metropolis and of transport more generally, upon which he has written many books and articles since his first, on the North London Railway, appeared in 1937. Much of his leisure has also been taken up in the service of the Museum of London (Governor from 1968 and Chairman from 1979) and of the Society of Antiquaries, of which he has been a Council Member, Treasurer (1971–87) and then President. The City University recognised his service and scholarship by bestowing upon him in 1987 the honorary degree of DLitt.

It is hoped that a new generation will be introduced to our work by this illustrated volume which the author dedicates

to his friend
Michael Robbins

Contents

List of Photographs

Foreword

This book, generously illustrated with photographs from the London Transport Museum's magnificent photographic archive, brings together the story of London Transport and its predecessors from the introduction of the horse bus in 1829 to the present day.

Specific aspects of London's transport history have been considered by a number of authors but for an overview the only source has been the two-volume *A History of London Transport*, jointly written by Professor Theo Barker and Michael Robbins. This monumental work, which ran to nearly 1,000 pages covering the period up to 1970, has long been out of print.

The intention of *Moving Millions* is to tell the story of London Transport from 1829 to the present day in an accessible way. No one could be better qualified to write it than Professor Barker. Apart from participating in the earlier work, he has produced a number of company histories and has written and broadcast widely on London's transport.

Theo's book is not a eulogy. It does not gloss over the problems which have beset the traveller in London in recent years and offers a very personal yet perceptive view of the unfolding of the story. For the newcomer to London's transport history and for the general reader, his book will serve as an excellent introduction to an essential aspect of London life.

Introduction

The fashionable part of the first passenger underground railway in the world: Baker Street station, seen here in 1863, is still in use and more readily recognisable after its recent renovation. The first stretch of line – part of the present Circle Line – ran from Farringdon Street to Paddington; it was soon extended, and provided an early morning workmen's service from 1864.

Ref. 16511

The larger towns become, the more important it is to be able to get about in them easily. The evolution of efficient and reliable transport becomes an increasingly vital factor in the complex process of urban growth. This is obvious in the case of freight, for no centre of commerce and industry can compete successfully with its rivals if it is disadvantaged financially by higher costs of moving goods. For the movement of people the role of transport is perhaps less obvious. It is no less crucial, however, for in larger cities it is impossible for everyone to live and work in the centre. People need to move out; and, as standards of living at home rise and working conditions also get better, they expect the transport link between the two – as well as travel for other purposes – also to improve. If it fails to do so, there are murmurings and letters to the editor. If it actually deteriorates, the complaints get louder and shriller. Radio and television become involved.

Pressure groups are formed and protest meetings held. If no effective action results, people start to move away and work elsewhere. Newcomers are not attracted. The city declines.

In London, steady improvement of passenger transport went hand in hand with the capital's very successful growth down to 1914 and continued between the wars. Then the pace of improvement visibly slackened until absolute decline set in during the early 1970s, if not a little earlier. The penalties of inadequate investment over several decades became evident not only in a host of ordinary ways obvious to almost everyone travelling by bus or Underground but also, most sensationally, in the tragic King's Cross fire. Serious public anxiety was aroused. At the time of writing some political action has already resulted, and there are indications of a will at least to make good the years of neglect. But there is a need to move on towards those further improvements that

Londoners now require and the city will need if it is to hold its own against competing business centres that have been investing in vastly improved public transport systems for decades.

The two-volume *A History of London Transport** has long been out of print. The aim of this book is to extract the essence of the story told there and to link it with the present in an attempt to explain why the great progress before the Second World War was not maintained; and, finally, in the light of this historical hindsight to suggest how public transport may be revived – to everyone's advantage.

THE STORY IN OUTLINE

During the nineteenth century London was the largest and most prosperous commercial and industrial centre on earth and the heart of the world's greatest empire. It already possessed a combination of constantly developing, privately owned, transport undertakings which showed considerable enterprise and initiative. London could boast the first steam Underground (1863) and the first electric tube railway (1890). When more electric tubes were built and the Underground was electrified – all by 1907 – Londoners enjoyed the most comfortable and speedy rapid transit system to be found in any great city. At about the same time the horse buses and horse trams disappeared from the streets and were replaced by larger, faster and much cheaper electric trams and motor buses covering longer routes, often running far out into open country which thus became attractive to property de-

ISLAND PLATFORM, STOCKWELL STATION.

Stockwell station in 1890. This was the original southern terminus of the City & South London Railway, the world's first underground electric line. The line was too small to be really profitable, however, and had soon to be rebuilt and partly re-routed. Other tube promoters learned from its example. Except for the Victoria and Jubilee Lines, all the present-day tubes in central London had been opened by 1907. Ref. 18526

* T.C. Barker and Michael Robbins, *A History of London Transport* Volume 1 (1963) The Nineteenth Century; Volume 2 (1974) The Twentieth Century to 1970. Paperback edition 1976.

It took several years to develop a dependable motor bus capable of repeatedly stopping and starting in London traffic. Success was achieved in 1909–10, and by the end of 1911 very few horse buses remained in service. The B-type motor bus shown here was the first reliable engine and chassis. The coachwork still owed much to the horse bus and the solid rubber tyres gave passengers a rather rough ride.   Ref. U13070

For the better-off there was, then as now, the cab. Motor cabs began to augment horse-drawn vehicles soon after 1900 but were little more than curiosities at first. The number plates of these two early versions, photographed by the Savoy Hotel in the Strand, show that they were produced soon after motor registration started in January 1904. As more taximetered motor cabs came on to the streets from 1907 onwards, the newcomers became known more popularly as taxis. By 1910 there were more taxis at work in London than there were horse-drawn hansoms and hackney coaches.   Ref. 21279

Electric tramways began to operate outside central London in 1901. For example, this spick and span London United tramcar initially ran west from Hammersmith and Shepherd's Bush; its driver and conductor are wearing impressive new uniforms. The service quickly built up a large traffic, and other private companies were also prompted to take over, rebuild, electrify and extend existing horse tramways in the outer districts. The London County Council, though slower to start, soon operated the most extensive system of all.   Ref. U24739

The motor bus gains and then loses popularity. (Above) Parliament Square in 1936, its traffic dominated by buses. With pneumatic tyres and covered top decks introduced during the later 1920s, they had become more comfortable and attracted a growing traffic. They could be hailed anywhere along the route and set down passengers at will. (Right) A photograph taken near the Elephant and Castle in 1966. During the 1950s other traffic grew and by the 1960s buses had to fight their way along the streets. As bus journey times became more unpredictable, passengers sought alternative forms of transport. Refs. 20046 and 19334

The first train arriving at Hendon Central station at 3 p.m. on 19 November 1923. It is clear how countrified the district still remained. The station was evidently not quite ready to receive its passengers – some of those on the platform were workmen.   Ref. U2345

velopers. The old horse cabs, too, were replaced by new motor taxis. Transport improvement went hand in hand with urban success and helped to maintain it.

This close association continued between the wars. Rail and bus services were considerably improved; and the extension of the Underground into open country, providing more rapid travel than the motor buses or electric trams, encouraged speculative building in the vicinity of the new railway stations. The electrification of the main-line railways, mostly south of the river, also generated additional traffic beyond the existing building frontier. The characteristic, easily recognisable, functional design of the stations on the Underground's extensions not only announced the arrival

of the new trains but also symbolised the architectural concern and environmental enterprise of its management. In central London, many of the original poky booking-office windows opening on to narrow and frequently shadowy passages were replaced by well-lit booking halls, often located in spacious concourses below street level. At the busier stations continuous escalators took the place of lifts.

The prewar leap forward, brought about by electric traction and the internal combustion engine, was thus sustained after 1918 by further steady development. All continued to be privately funded, though government guarantees were required for the raising of capital at advantageous rates of in-

terest. London greatly benefited as a commercial centre. So did the travelling public.

Transport developments, both before and after the First World War, also played an important part in the improvement of housing conditions by enabling many poorer people to follow the better-off into the suburbs. This process began with the introduction to London of workmen's fares on the steam Underground in 1864, a year after its opening, but was greatly accelerated as the century progressed. Many working people who had previously walked could now afford to ride, and to ride longer distances. Some of the worst central slums began to be cleared and their inhabitants were able to move away from their

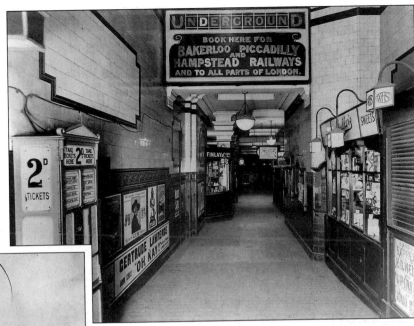

Style on the extended Underground: (i) (left) the booking hall at Arnos Grove station, opened in September 1932. Ref. U21647

(ii) (above) Piccadilly Circus station in 1928, before its renovation, with the old booking office windows in the background; (below) the new booking hall below street level in 1929. Refs. H/16155 and U12002

The new suburbia made possible by public transport developments: Kenton in 1934.
Aerofilms

London Transport's outstanding postwar development was the Victoria Line, opened by the Queen in 1969. Its authorisation by the Government had resulted not from London's needs but from fears of growing unemployment hundreds of miles away.
Ref. 24801

cramped and crowded streets. More people came to live in houses with their own gardens and to breathe fresher air.

Since 1945 there has been no such steady transport progress. True, London has seen the building of the Victoria Line, its stunted successor the Jubilee Line, and the Docklands Light Railway. But this compares unfavourably with the steady advances of the previous 45 years – a time when the country as a whole, and London in particular, commanded considerably fewer economic resources.

Earlier lack of station maintenance is everywhere evident from the belated and prolonged efforts to catch up. Escalators and lifts are frequently out of service. Because of the success of travelcards and an increase of 50 per cent in the Underground's passenger traffic between 1984 and 1989, trains and stations in central London are often disagreeably congested. Journey times are unpredictable, and travellers need to allow much longer for a given journey than they once did now fire regulations cause unexpected stoppages. The lot of the Underground traveller is not at present a happy one.

On the buses, the difficulty of providing a good standard of service has been far worse, not least because, as it does not control its road, London Transport has been even less its own master. The increase in private cars and commercial vehicles has not only deprived the buses of traffic but has also so congested the centre of the city for much of the day that journey times are even more unpredictable than on the Underground. London Transport's total traffic by road fell spectacularly from a peak of nearly 4,000 million journeys in 1948 to a mere 1,200 million journeys in 1988–89. (To be more exact, excluding coaches and country buses from the peak figure, as they have been from the later one, the total has fallen from 3.65 thousand million.) London's buses now carry only 7 per cent of commuters during the morning rush.

There are clear signs, however, that the long, slow tide of decline is turning. The station renovations that have caused so much misery on the Underground will in time bring their benefits, and large capital allocations have been made for further improvement. Authorisation has been given for the Jubilee Line to be extended eastwards, although not on the route originally proposed, and other east–west links are under active consideration. Bus

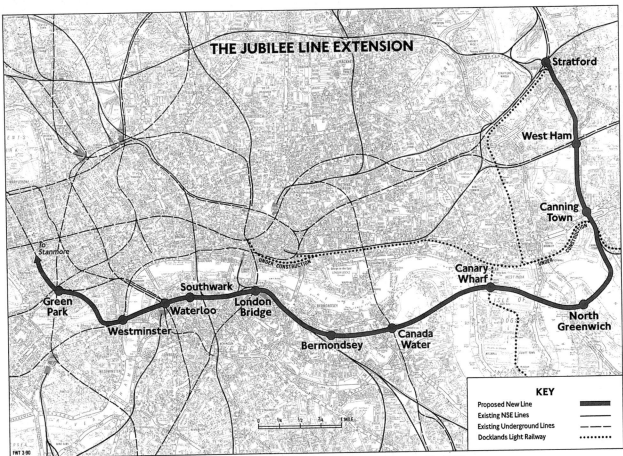

The proposed route for the Jubilee Line extension approved in 1989.

Crowded trains and escalators under repair pose a problem to the modern-day commuter. Refs. 24804 and 24803

operation has been broken down into more manageable divisions and some of the mileage put out to competitive tender. The whole organisation of London Transport has been divisionalised, with a central holding company overseeing a family of subsidiaries.

A huge task of modernisation and expansion lies ahead and the biggest nettle of all has still to be grasped: to find a way of dealing with road congestion, which is absolutely essential if the buses are to flow freely once again. And this they must do if they are to regain their old position of providing most of the profits that once enabled London Transport to flourish and grow.

Public opinion is becoming aroused, however, and politicians are starting to take notice. It is hoped that this book may provide helpful evidence and useful arguments in the growing debate.

Part One

Horses and Steam

District Loco No. 10 at West Brompton station, District Line, in 1876.
Ref. U4650

THE ARRIVAL OF THE OMNIBUS

By 1800 London's population was approaching a million. It was the main industrial centre of the nation, and probably of the world, though manufacturing was concentrated in small workshops and attracted less public attention than the few steam-powered factories recently set up elsewhere in the country. More important, it was the country's major port and centre of banking and insurance.

As the businesses in the centre kept on growing, there was less space for people to live there. Businesses could pay higher rents, and increasingly took over the central sites. People who could afford to do so moved out to live in the suburbia of the day. The wealthiest had their own private carriages; others used hackney coaches, limited in number by the authorities and possessing sole rights to ply for hire in the central streets.

The beginnings of public transport as we now know it are to be traced to the short-stage coaches which, a directory of 1768 tells us, were already running out to the villages of Kensington (14 coaches a day) and Hammersmith (ten a day). Hourly services ran to the City from three separate termini in Islington, and almost every nearby village had at least one coach a day.

All these vehicles were horse-drawn and, because horses were expensive to feed and maintain and their working life in traffic relatively short, fares were quite high. Costs were increased further by mileage duties, payable on the number of horses per vehicle and the number of passengers for which each was licensed, irrespective of the number actually carried on each journey. Only the better-off could afford to ride. Working people, when displaced by new offices or workshops, had to

walk; more often than not, they were crowded into congested dwellings close to their employment.

As London grew – its population neared 1½ million in 1821 and 1¾ million ten years later – so more individual operators put their vehicles on the road to meet the growing demand. By 1825, 418 of them ran out from the City and perhaps another 200 from the West End, some 600 in all – a fifth of all the stage coaches then licensed throughout the country. The extent of the built-up area is shown in the map on pages 14 and 15.

Stage coaches, though suitable for travel between towns, were far from

George Shillibeer (1797–1866), who gained a place in the Dictionary of National Biography *for introducing the horse omnibus to London. He could not withstand the rough and tumble of business, however, and went bankrupt. After a spell in a debtors' prison, he invented a new type of funeral carriage and made good at last in the less lively business of undertaking.* Refs. U5441, 3052/63 and H/6966

ideal for city work, even when adapted by the addition of a dickey space at the back which passengers could reach by climbing a short ladder instead of having to clamber on to the roof. Some, indeed, called to collect their passengers from

home in the morning and returned them there at the end of the day. The more picking up *en route* the short-stage coach undertook, however, the less suitable it became. What was needed was a box on wheels that could be easily entered and would shelter most passengers from the weather.

Although there had been earlier attempts to introduce such a vehicle to London, it had not found favour. Now, however, it arrived as an import from France thanks to the initiative of George Shillibeer, a London coachbuilder who also had 'an establishment for the sale of carriages' in Paris. In 1828, the Prefect of Police had given permission for *L'Entreprise des Omnibus* to put 100 of its box-like vehicles on ten routes running across densely populated central Paris, obviously intended to pick up and set down frequently on each journey. Shillibeer, able to witness personally their immediate success, was quick to put such a vehicle, built to his own design to carry 20 passengers and drawn by three horses, on London's busiest route. He at first proposed to put his new product on the streets under the more English name of *Economist*; but *Omnibus*, the latest from Paris, proved more popular.

Shillibeer's omnibus started to run between Paddington Green and the Bank on 4 July 1829. Although an hour was allowed for the journey of five miles, it was sometimes achieved in 40 minutes. The venture was a success and Shillibeer put on more omnibuses. So did his rivals, who wisely ran somewhat smaller vehicles accommodating 12 passengers, pulled by two horses instead of three, and therefore paying a lower rate of mileage duty.

Unrestricted bus competition has never been able to survive for long. Sooner or later (usually sooner) the competitors have to get together, form

SHILLIBEER'S OMNIBUS.

A New Carriage on the Parisian Mode, for the Conveyance of Inside Passengers from PADDINGTON to the BANK.
Established by G. Shillibeer, Coach Builder &c. No. 12 Bury Str. Bloomsbury Square.

OMNIBUS.

G. SHILLIBEER, induced by the universal admiration the above Vehicles called forth at Paris, has commenced running one upon the Parisian mode, from PADDINGTON to the BANK.

The superiority of this Carriage over the ordinary Stage Coaches, for comfort and safety, must be obvious, all the Passengers being Inside, and the Fare charged from Paddington to the Bank being One Shilling, and from Islington to the Bank or Paddington, only Sixpence.

The Proprietor begs to add, that a person of great respectability attends his Vehicle as Conductor; and every possible attention will be paid to the accommodation of Ladies and Children.

Hours of Starting :—From Paddington Green to the Bank, at 9, 12, 3, 6, and 8 o'clock ; from the Bank to Paddington, at 10, 1, 4, 7, and 9 o'clock.

DERRING'S PATENT LIGHT SUMMER

*London in 1820 (population 1½ million)
stretched from east to west rather than from
north to south, although tongues of building
reached outwards along the main roads in all
directions. Short-stage coaches served all
these areas. At that time the busiest route ran
along the City Road to the Angel and then
along the New Road – the present-day
Pentonville, Euston and Marylebone Roads –
to Paddington. Regent's Park was already in
existence, and Lord's had moved to its
present site. Hackney coaches still enjoyed
monopoly rights in the busy central district,
and short-stage coaches were not allowed to
ply for hire there.*

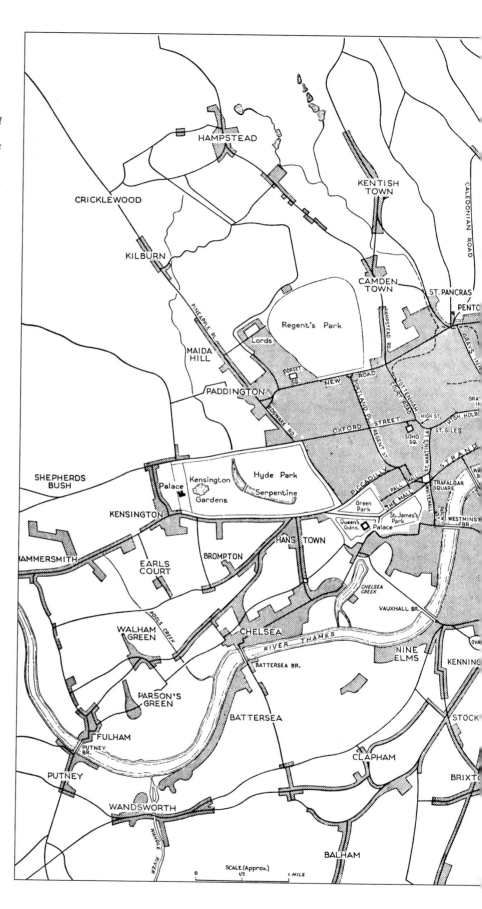

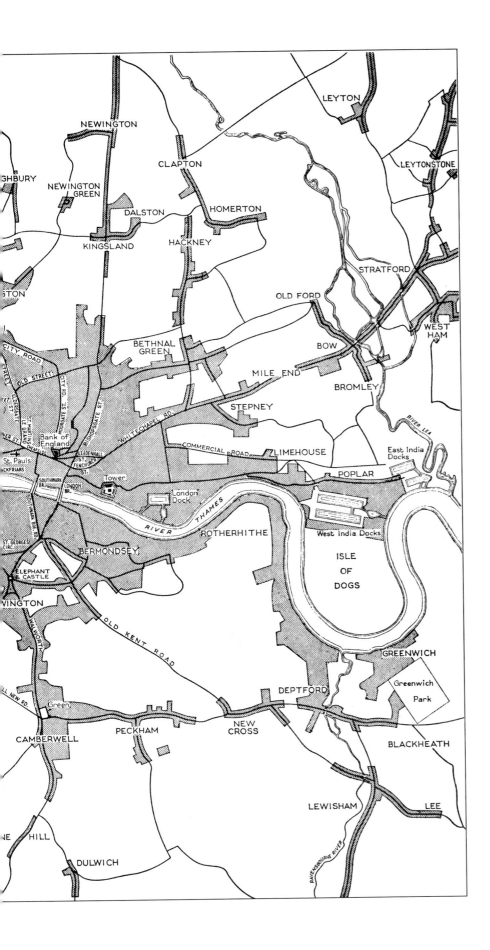

THE STAR of CAMBRIDGE.

Two London street scenes in the 1830s showing (above) a traditional stage coach leaving the Belle Sauvage Inn and (top right) the Blackheath stage coach with dickey space at the back. Horse omnibuses are shown in both views.   Refs. 1700 and U23886C

From 1832 onwards more hackney coaches were allowed on the streets, and greater competition developed. An improved form of two-wheel cabriolet, the hansom, proved very popular, as did a new type of four-wheeler, the brougham. This photograph, taken in Northumberland Avenue later in the century, shows a hansom cab of the kind often used by Conan Doyle's Sherlock Holmes, a four-wheeler following.   Ref. 19952

an association to limit the number of vehicles on a particular route, agree fares and allocate times to each bus. In September 1831 the various operators on the Paddington route agreed that 33 of the vehicles then running along it should be withdrawn and the remaining 57 should run a three-minute service with allocated times. Inspectors were posted along the road to see that this agreement was carried out. If interlopers

of tradespeople whose finances cannot admit of the accommodation of a hackney coach and therefore necessitated to lose that time in walking which might be beneficially devoted to business at home'. The new omnibuses were given freedom of the central streets from 5 January 1832. Associations were soon formed on the various routes.

As a *quid pro quo*, the limit to the number of London's hackney carriages

the duty was at last levied on the vehicle itself rather than the number of passengers for which it was licensed. The carrying capacity was increased from 13 or 16 to 24 or 25 by adding two seats lengthwise on the roof. With these new double-deckers fares between stages were reduced to twopence or threepence.

It was in each bus crew's interest to pick up as many passengers as possible for, if the vehicles were not owner-operated, the crews were paid to some extent by results. The conductor's job, in addition to collecting fares from alighting passengers, was to keep the vehicle as full as he could. He achieved his objective by cajoling and enticing the hesitant into his brightly painted omnibus as he stood on a step at the back. The driver, for his part, dawdled if his bus was only half full, holding up his whip significantly.

There were soon complaints of delayed journeys and traffic obstruction. In 1838 legislation obliged all drivers and conductors to register their names, addresses and ages for purposes of identification. Each was given a metal badge which displayed his licence number so that he could be prosecuted if necessary.

To sit on the front edge of the roof by the driver (or coachman, as he liked to be called) was always popular. Following the introduction of the new method of levying mileage duty in 1842, two seats were placed lengthways on the roof (they were soon christened knifeboard seats), reached by a vertical ladder at the back of the vehicle. The London double-decker had arrived.
Ref. 15275

not in the association tried to run 'pirate' buses, they were 'nursed' – that is, several association vehicles ran in front of them to pick up all the fares. Within the association, however, individual operators were quite at liberty to expand their businesses by buying the 'times' of others.

By the early 1830s, there was a strong move to abolish the hackney coach monopoly so that omnibuses could work the lucrative central streets. Shillibeer was among those who strongly supported this, urging the particular advantages for 'the middling class

was also removed. More competition developed in that trade, too, as more vehicles were licensed. Two-wheel cabriolets ('cabs') proved particularly popular. By the mid-1840s 2,450 two-wheelers and 200 four-wheelers were licensed in London.

By 1839 620 omnibuses had been licensed, each to carry 15 passengers. Two hundred short-stage coaches still came in from the outskirts. The mileage duty had been reduced in 1832 and 1839. In 1842 it was reduced again, from twopence-halfpenny to threehalfpence per mile; more importantly,

STEAM ON RIVER AND LAND

Steamboats began to ply on the Thames in 1815, over a decade before any serious attempts were made to use steam power to carry Londoners by land. Sizeable traffic was generated by these vessels, which could carry several hundred passengers at a time and charged low fares. By the early 1830s the service to Greenwich ran every half hour in winter (continuing after dark) and every quarter of an hour in summer. Smaller steamboats, carry-

"OMNIBUS LIFE IN LONDON."—FROM A PICTURE BY W. M. EGLEY.—IN THE BRITISH INSTITUTION.—see supplement, page 571.

An engraving made from a painting by
W M Egley, published in the Illustrated
London News, *shows that the small horse*
bus could become very full inside, although
everyone did have a seat! Ref. 24764

ing up to 120 passengers, began to ply between London and Westminster Bridges in 1837; they took between 15 and 30 minutes over the journey and charged fourpence. By 1843, eight steamboats were providing a 15-minute service between London Bridge and Chelsea, carrying more than two million passengers a year; the fare all the way was soon cut to twopence. A new service between London Bridge and the Adelphi charged as little as a halfpenny. These were the lowest fares available on any form of transport in London at that time, and in the mid-1850s 15,000 people came into London every day by this means.

The steamboats were well able to support the relatively massive steam engines of the day. On the streets of London, however, the engines were too heavy. Yet there were strong incentives to encourage their use, for London was an important centre of the country's steam engine manufacture. And though too weighty for use on ordinary roads, the locomotive was as great a success on specially built railway track in London as elsewhere.

London's first railway was opened between Deptford and Spa Road, Bermondsey, on 8 February 1836. It was part of a 3¾-mile line being built between London and Greenwich, which on 14 December 1836 reached an inner terminus on the south side of London Bridge, conveniently situated for commuters to walk into the City. The line was completed to Greenwich on 29 December 1838. The original two tracks ran on a viaduct, thereby minimising the amount of land required and keeping the trains well above the existing property although, as the early advertisement on page 22 shows, the viaduct also ran into undeveloped open country. The advertisement shows too that the fares

H S Melville, del.

THE FLEET OF THE CITY ST

Edwin Jewitt, lith.

I BOATS PASSING IN REVIEW ORDER OFF CHELSEA

were higher than wage earners could afford and, as with the buses, the first trains of the day started too late for them. There were, however, specially low-priced excursions on public holidays. In 1843 the return fares had to be reduced, because of steamboat competition, to one shilling for first- and ten-pence for second-class passengers respectively; third-class passengers paid a single fare of fourpence. The line carried more than two million people in 1844.

The original terminus at London Bridge consisted of little more than uncovered platforms and a handsome pair of iron gates. In 1838, however, the London & Croydon Railway joined the original London & Greenwich Line to take advantage of this well-situated terminus and London & Brighton trains also started to run in there (1841). A new functional building – with an Italianate campanile feature – was erected and came into full use by 1845. Traffic was generated down the new line from stations at New Cross, Forest Gate, and onwards to Croydon and beyond. Here, together with the first part of the London & Southampton Railway opened from Woking to Nine Elms, Vauxhall, are to be found the humble beginnings of what later became the Southern Railway and, more recently, the part of Network South East that has generated such a huge volume of tightly packed commuter traffic.

North of the river, the London & Blackwall Railway was opened for traffic between the Minories and Blackwall on 8 July 1840 and through to Fenchurch Street on 7 August 1841. The new line was about the same length as the London & Greenwich and was also built on a viaduct; it too was in time joined by other lines because of its convenient City terminus. Cable-hauled at first, this railway cut out the long river bend

round the Isle of Dogs and offered severe competition to the steamboats which, in due course, fed much of their Woolwich traffic on to it. It carried two million people in 1841 at single fares of eightpence and fourpence according to class.

Other railways were being built in London. The main lines north of the river reached Euston in 1837, an earlier station near Paddington in 1838 (the present one originates from 1854), Shoreditch in 1849 (Liverpool Street dates from 1874–75) and King's Cross in 1852, a temporary station at Maiden Lane having been used for the previous two years. South of the river, while

London Bridge gained more traffic from the south and south-east, trains from the south-west were brought forward from Nine Elms to Waterloo Road in 1848. During the Railway Mania of the mid-1840s, various proposals were made to extend railways into central London. These, however, were vetoed by a Royal Commission which concluded that the existing peripheral stations kept down road congestion by distributing the street traffic they generated.

The London & North Western Railway, which owned the line into Euston, needed direct access to the docks near Blackwall for its heavy freight traffic from the north. A subsidiary was formed

The London Bridge Railway terminus in 1845. Ref. 3052/59

to construct a railway from its main line at Camden Town eastward through Islington, Hackney and Bow, round what was then the outer limit of the built-up area. It was soon realised that, with a junction to the London & Blackwall, extra passenger traffic could be generated if a rapid rail service was run into Fenchurch Street. Passenger trains began to run into the City along this roundabout route in 1850. In the first half of 1851, running every 15 minutes, they carried 1¾ million people at single fares of sixpence and fourpence.

In 1853 the trains of the North London Railway (as it then came to be called) also started to run westwards to Kew and beyond, first using the main line to West London Junction near Kensal Green and, from 1860, along a new line through Kentish Town (Gospel Oak), Hampstead Heath, Finchley Road and Edgware Road (Kilburn).

The early success of this venture outside central London focused interest on the possibilities of another line farther in, underneath an established residential area. The initiative arose from two quarters. The City Corporation was keen to remove its cattle market, unhealthy industries and insanitary dwellings from the Fleet valley; moreover Charles Pearson, the City Solicitor, appreciated that railways could run trains at very cheap fares which would enable at least the better-off working people to follow the middle classes into the suburbs. In addition, there were entrepreneurs who believed that a railway connecting with the Fleet Valley line could be built under the busy Euston and Marylebone Roads to Paddington, joining the Great Western Railway there and the Great Northern at

Cable traction on the London and Blackwall Railway. Ref. 24748

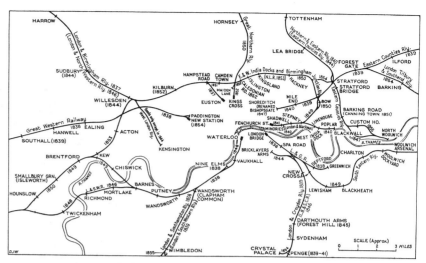

Railway construction in London up to 1855.

The North London Railway crossing the Great Northern Railway on a viaduct near Maiden Lane, 1851.   Ref. 19491

Charles Pearson, the City Solicitor. He was a strong supporter of an underground railway which, he realised, would enable workmen to travel more cheaply to their employment in London. Ref. H/13989

The 'cut and cover' tunnels of the Metropolitan Railway under construction in the Marylebone Road. Ref. U13799

King's Cross, enabling some of their trains to run into the City. Rapid transit would be provided both for passengers along the route and, by a station nearby, for those arriving at Euston, where the main-line company had enough long-distance passengers and was not anxious to develop suburban traffic by a direct rail connection.

It took the whole of the 1850s for the sponsors to convince the street authorities that the railway would save them road costs, Parliament that it was possible to build locomotives that could consume their own smoke, the City Corporation that its financial support was not only in its own environmental interest but also crucial to the ultimate

success of the whole scheme, and the investing public that enough passengers could be persuaded to descend into the damp and no doubt rat-infested tunnels for the Metropolitan Railway ever to make a profit. Building at last began towards the end of 1859, however.

The section from the Fleet valley under Mount Pleasant was tunnelled, but the rest, under Euston and Marylebone Roads – still London's main traffic artery – was built by 'cut and cover', by digging up the road, excavating a cutting in which the railway was laid, and putting the road back on top. 'Blow holes' were left at points in the middle of the road to enable fumes and steam to escape from the new railway.

THE WORLD'S LARGEST OMNIBUS UNDERTAKING

Extra omnibuses were put into service in 1851 to carry the crowds who came to London for the Great Exhibition. But when they all went home again the capital was left with too many vehicles. Competition intensified: fares fell to as low as a penny, and some proprietors were driven out of business.

In 1854 war between Russia and Turkey made the price of horse feed soar; later that year vehicle inspection by the Metropolitan Police was instituted. Both increased the operating costs of the omnibuses. Several of the major proprietors formed a committee in the following year and urged the Chancellor of the Exchequer to cut the mileage duty, arguing that their business had been barely profitable since 1851. The duty was reduced from three-halfpence to one penny per vehicle per mile in June 1855.

Meanwhile Paris was showing the London industry another way out of its difficulties. Company promoters, supported by bankers and the *Commission Municipale*, merged the Paris omnibuses into a single *Compagnie Générale des Omnibus* early in 1855, just in time to profit from traffic generated by the International Exhibition held in Paris that year. The merger proved most successful for the bus business and the promoters then looked in the direction of London for further gains. Some London proprietors had grown considerably in importance by purchasing more buses and the 'times' that went with them, and three of the largest, who together owned over 100 of the 810 omnibuses then licensed, were promised lucrative managerial posts in the proposed merged company and a share of the profits. Not surprisingly, they welcomed the French overtures. The *Compagnie Générale des Omnibus de Londres* was registered in Paris in December 1855 with a capital of 25 million francs (£1 million) divided into 250,000 100-franc shares; 200,000 of these were issued at

PROSPECTUS

OF THE

Compagnie Générale des Omnibus de Londres

(THE LONDON GENERAL OMNIBUS COMPANY).

Established in Paris, under Acts of the 4th and 17th December, 1855, as a "*Société en commandite*, by which the liability of each Shareholder is limited to the amount subscribed.

CAPITAL:

TWENTY-FIVE MILLIONS OF FRANCS—ONE MILLION STERLING,

In 250,000 Shares of 100 Francs, or £4 each.

In Two Series.—The First, 200,000 Shares (£800,000.)
The Second, 50,000 Shares (£200,000.)

The First Series only will be issued at present.

Gerants of the Company.

MACNAMARA, CARTERET, WILLING & Co.

Managers in London.

Messrs. JOHN WILSON.
  ,,   JOHN BARBER.
  ,,   RICHARD HARTLEY.
  ,,   JOHN TREVETT.

Members of the Council of Surveillance.

ROBERT KEATING, Esq., M.P., Director of the London & County Bank....LONDON.
LE COMTE DE LANTIVY..PARIS.
VACOSSIN, Administrateur de la Compagnie d'Assurance l'Urbaine.........PARIS.
FRÉDÉRIC TOCHÉ, Banquier ....PARIS.
EDWIN CHADWICK, Esq., C.B.....................................LONDON.
AUGUSTIN DUBOIS, Administrateur des Forges de Montataire............PARIS.
MARZIOU, Directeur-Gérant de l'Union Maritime ....PARIS.
TH. HARRISSON, Esq..LONDON.

Bankers.

In Paris....MESSRS. GREENE & Co.
In London.. { THE LONDON AND COUNTY BANK.
           { MESSRS. ROBARTS, CURTIS & Co.

Solicitors.

In Paris....MR. PETIT BERGONZ, Avoué au Tribunal de Première Instance.
In London....MESSRS. WILKINSON, GURNEY & Co.

THE undoubted advantages produced by the amalgamation of the Omnibuses of Paris, have originated the plan of concentrating, in one Great Enterprise, the several Associations now working the Omnibuses of London.

*A knifeboard bus in 1891. The temporary
signs suggest that its former owner was
recently taken over by the LGOC.*
Ref. U29253C

(Right and below) LGOC stables. (Top photo)
Ref. U58323. *(Bottom photo) Courtesy of*
Mr H. C. Woodyard.   Ref. 24440

Bus crews were highly paid, but grossly overworked. Uniform jackets and caps were not introduced by the LGOC until 1910.   Ref. H/6203

the outset, mainly to French investors.

The London merger proved much more difficult to organise than that in Paris, partly because no *Commission Municipale* was involved and partly because there was much English hostility to what was seen as a takeover by the old enemy (even though France was at the time temporarily an ally). The London collaborators, however, were well placed to bring pressure to bear on other members in the route associations, which they dominated. Offers of £510 per vehicle, which represented a high price for goodwill at such a time of difficulty in the omnibus business, clinched the deal, sweetened in some cases by offers of district managerships or other jobs. By December 1856, 600 omnibuses had been acquired. The remaining 200 or so maintained their

independence but ran in close association with the new company.

It was not helped by its French origins, however, especially when the Crimean War ended and France became the old enemy again. The company's registration was transferred to London at the beginning of 1859, and the London General Omnibus Company – 'the General' – was thereafter seen to be British. The 100-franc shares were exchanged for new shares worth an equal sum in English currency (£4). The French kept their major financial interest for a year or two longer, but they no longer exercised any real control: only four of the 12 newly appointed directors were French, and shareholders' meetings were now held in London. For another 55 years, however, the reports and balance sheets continued to

be printed in French as well as English.

The creation of the LGOC had been costly. Its French sponsors seem to have pocketed over £100,000 for their efforts, £32,500 was spent on publicity and brokerage, and the company had had to pay dearly for its 600 omnibuses. Economies were urgently needed and were soon effected, especially in the purchase and processing of horse feed, the most costly item of all. By April 1857, steam-driven machinery was being used at the Spitalfields depot (and later at Paddington, Chelsea and Highbury) for preparing grain, cutting straw and bruising oats for the company's horses. New stables were built and veterinary surgeons appointed.

An attempt was made to introduce prepaid vouchers for bus travel, but these were soon discontinued. Nor were tickets introduced – nor, indeed, any other means of counting passengers so that conductors' takings could be checked. Conductors continued to supplement their wages by some of the day's takings. An LGOC official claimed in the 1860s that this then cost the company £25,000 a year; but the new managers, formerly the old proprietors, were not prepared to change the system. They knew roughly what the takings of an omnibus on a particular route should be. If the conductor took more than this sum, he was allowed to pocket the difference, but if he was greedy, he risked dismissal. He was expected to share these extra takings with the driver who, in turn, looked after the horse-keeper and waterman who changed or fed the horses at the terminus (which was often at a public house) while the crew took a few minutes' rest. Conductors and drivers could earn from 35 shillings to two pounds a week, or even more, and were thus among the highest-paid of working men. They had, however, to begin working their vehicle as early as 7.30 in the morning (crews reporting 20 minutes before that); the first vehicles out did not return until around 11 at night and the later ones came in after midnight. They worked seven days a week, an unpaid day's leave being granted now and again if it suited the company. The pay was so good, however, that LGOC's general manager could later claim: 'When we want six conductors, we often have 60 or 80 candidates.'

The crews worked far longer hours than the horses. A two-horse London omnibus required 11 or 12 horses to keep it on the road all day, each team being changed after a few journeys and having frequent rest days. Spare horses were needed in case of sickness.

THE BEGINNINGS OF THE RAIL NETWORK

Traffic jams, already familiar, became an increasingly common feature of London life. No doubt Gustave Doré employed artist's licence when he drew a particularly classic example, but the hundreds of horse omnibuses can scarcely have helped matters. They converged upon the central thoroughfares and mingled with the hackney carriages (1,500 licensed in 1830, and 3,000 in 1850) and the multitude of goods vehicles of all sorts. Apart from New Oxford Street, built in the 1840s to link Tottenham Court Road with Holborn, and Cannon Street, built in the 1850s, no important new thoroughfares were constructed in the centre at that time. Holborn Viaduct, which saved the descent into the Fleet valley on a major east–west artery, was not opened until 1869.

Road congestion was greatly eased when railways from the south were bridged across the river to termini on its northern bank. A complete new railway, the London, Chatham & Dover, ran through north Kent via St Mary Cray into the new terminus, christened Victoria, in 1860. The London, Brighton & South Coast (LBSC) also reached there

A City Thoroughfare *by Gustave Doré.*   Ref. 24752

Two of the four new termini opened north of the river in the 1860s, which saved London Bridge passengers from the south from having to travel onward from there by road, and delivered them close to their destination: (above) Charing Cross in 1864, (left) Cannon Street in 1866. Refs. 3052/10 and 24201

Ludgate Hill *by Gustave Doré.*

that year and built its own station immediately adjoining. This rivalry spurred the South Eastern to extend its lines from London Bridge across the river to termini at Charing Cross (1864) and Cannon Street (1866). In response its new competitor, the London, Chatham & Dover, drove a particularly expensive branch north from Herne Hill to Blackfriars. That spectacular eyesore, the

(second) and threepence (third) with returns for ninepence, sixpence and fivepence.

Parliamentary powers had already been gained to extend it eastwards to Moorgate Street in the City, within easy walking distance of the Bank. Trains started to run there at the end of December 1865. An extension westwards used the Great Western main line

needed to handle it all.

A committee of the House of Lords was set up in 1863 to study the various proposed London railway schemes. In the following year a joint committee of both Houses advised that the existing pioneer stretch of underground, already accommodating the termini at King's Cross and Paddington by direct rail links and, to some extent, Euston (though not by direct link) should be extended at both ends to form an 'inner circuit' to serve the other main-line termini, built or to be built, north of the river. The Metropolitan accordingly sought powers to continue its line eastwards from Moorgate Street and round the City in one direction and, in the other, from Paddington via Bayswater, Notting Hill Gate, and High Street, Kensington, to Brompton (South Kensington). Another company, the Metropolitan District, was formed to link Brompton with the Metropolitan's City extension, serving the new termini at Victoria, Charing Cross and Cannon Street. The Metropolitan District was also to build west from Brompton alongside the Metropolitan's tracks to Gloucester Road and then on westwards through the fields of Earl's Court.

A trial trip in contractors' wagons in May 1862, eight months before the new Metropolitan Railway was opened; the trip was no doubt arranged in order to raise further capital to extend the line. Mr and Mrs Gladstone are said to be in the party. The photograph was taken during a stop at Edgware Road.   Ref. 17451

bridge across the bottom of Ludgate Hill (also drawn by Doré) and the terminus there (1864–65) was followed by that at Holborn Viaduct (1874).

The opening of the underground, most important in its own right as the world's first underground passenger railway, and its extension, must be seen as part of this more general spread of London's railway facilities. The first 3½-mile stretch, from Farringdon Street to Paddington, was opened on Saturday 10 January 1863. It was an immediate success and carried 26,500 passengers per day during its first six months at fares of sixpence (first class), fourpence

for a mile or so out of Paddington and then took a new railway (the Hammersmith & City) through fields south of Porto Bello and Notting Barn Farms, reaching a terminus near the north side of Hammersmith Broadway. It was opened on 13 June 1864, the first of several branches. The second, to Swiss Cottage, followed in 1868.

Suburban trains from the Great Northern line out of King's Cross from as far away as Hatfield and Hitchin, which also connected with the new underground, developed such a large traffic over the Metropolitan into the City that two additional tracks were

The Metropolitan's western section was opened from Paddington to Gloucester Road on 1 October 1868 and to Brompton (South Kensington) on the following 24 December, when the Metropolitan District's line from Westminster was also opened. Taking advantage of the newly built Victoria Embankment, the Metropolitan District reached Blackfriars by 30 May 1870 and trains eventually ran into a station at the corner of Cannon Street (misleadingly called Mansion House) on 3 July 1871. (The intended Circle remained a horseshoe for some time: apart from the Metropolitan's extension from

(Left) The second Clerkenwell Tunnel and the so-called 'widened lines', opened in 1868; they were built to accommodate Great Northern trains and those from the Midland Railway, whose own terminus at St Pancras was opened in that year. Both these railways developed a large traffic from the northern suburbs and home counties into the City. The widened lines connected with the London, Chatham & Dover Railway to the south, thus enabling trains to be run across London. This through-service stopped during the First World War, but was reopened as Thameslink in 1988. (Below) Farringdon Street station after the new lines had been added.   Refs. H/3958 and H/3957

The beginning of the Circle Line: the extension of the Metropolitan Railway westwards from Paddington (above). Continuing the tunnel along Praed Street about 1866; (left) Paddington–Praed Street station under construction. Refs. 17438 and 17440

Bayswater station: (left) nearing completion, (below) the frontage of the station after the Metropolitan District Railway's opening to Westminster on Christmas Eve 1868.
Refs. 17441 and 20719

Steam underground: a train arriving at Charing Cross station (now called Embankment) a decade after the completion of the Circle.   Ref. H/10485

The Metropolitan District Railway built the section of the new Underground from Gloucester Road to Westminster (1868), and was fortunate in having the new Victoria Embankment for its extension eastwards. Navvies pose for their photograph outside Somerset House as they dig towards Mansion House station about 1869.   Ref. 19777

The Metropolitan ran under Leinster Gardens in fashionable Bayswater. Dummy frontages were put up at numbers 23 and 24 to hide its existence.   Refs. 19493 and 18725

river and the underground greatly reduced steamboat traffic through London itself. Summer excursions became the steamboats' mainstay, but in September 1878 an appalling disaster befell the *Princess Alice* when she collided with a collier and sank while returning from one of these trips. More than 700 people were drowned. The calamity hastened the demise of the London Steamboat Company Ltd into which the existing firms had merged three years before.

Moorgate Street to Aldgate in 1876, the cost of the City part of the scheme was prohibitive. Its completion was not achieved for another eight years, the underground in the process obtaining an exit eastwards under Whitechapel High Street. Trains started running round the Circle on 17 September 1884.)

The 1860s was thus a most significant decade in the history of London's transport, with this massive investment in steam railways laying the foundations of a transport network that is still benefiting Londoners. The finance all came from private sources, although its investment was to some extent guided by Parliament. Quick and efficient rail travel enabled the middle classes to commute from areas that had not yet been opened up by the horse omnibus or that lay beyond bus routes. Railways eased congestion in the central streets and, as we shall see, their fares became so low that some working people began to use them to travel to their employment.

The railways put an end to regular steamboat services to places like Gravesend and Richmond, and the building of the new main-line termini north of the

HORSE TRAMWAYS

Because the rolling resistance of iron wheels on smooth rails is much less than that of omnibus wheels on ordinary road surfaces, the simple device of a tramway enabled two horses to pull a larger vehicle and carry more passengers. Spreading operating costs over 48 passengers instead of 24 made it possible to charge lower fares. Although street authorities' sanction had to be obtained to lay the track, they were in turn saved the cost of maintaining part of the road. Fixed costs were relatively small.

While the idea of London's omnibuses came from France, that of its tramways came from the United States where these street railways (as they were there more accurately described) had existed from the 1830s and had begun to spread from the 1850s. In most American towns, however, roads were in a far worse condition than those of the main European cities. The Americans used a type of step rail, the vertical part of which protruded above the road surface. Vehicles other than tramcars could run upon their flat surfaces.

In 1861, George Francis Train attempted to introduce this American type of rail on three routes in London (along part of Bayswater Road, along

The Princess Alice *disaster, 3 September 1878.*   Ref. 24767

VICTORIA ST (East end) . . . . . 1861.

A false start: G F Train's Victoria Street tramway (1861).   Ref. H/8731

Victoria Street and from Westminster Bridge to Kennington). But there was such an outcry that the trials had to be abandoned. In any event, the attention of investors was then monopolised by the railway boom. Soon, however, the cheaper tramway, using an acceptable form of rail laid flush with the road surface so as not to impede crossing traffic, came rapidly into its own and generated a large traffic at very reasonable fares.

In 1869 Parliament allowed three companies to lay their lines along a few specific routes, two south of the river and one in the East End, all running down wide roads and none of them in

fashionable neighbourhoods. The first vehicles of the Metropolitan Street Tramways Company (later to form part of London Tramways), imported from America, began to run down Brixton Road from Brixton to Kennington Church on 2 May 1870, the route being completed to Westminster Bridge Road on 5 October. A second company opened a line from Blackheath Hill to New Cross, and a third built along the Mile End Road between Whitechapel and Bow Churches. All were highly successful and further lines were approved, all franchised for 21 years with repurchase by the road authority at scrap value after that time. No lines were allowed in the

City, however, apart from a brief stretch to Finsbury Square, nor in the West End as far out as Shepherd's Bush. The omnibuses were therefore able to maintain their traffic, despite higher fares, because they alone ran in the central streets and took passengers nearer to their ultimate destination. But in 1875 the new trams were carrying almost as much traffic as the LGOC (48.9 million and 49.7 million journeys respectively, though to the former must be added those carried by its associates). In the 1870s, that is to say, the new tramcars were making a major contribution, much as the new railways had done in the previous decade.

(Right) London's tramways in 1875.
Ref. 16221

(Below) The beginnings of a great success: an artist's impression of one of the first horse trams, imported from America, at the gallop on the Westminster Bridge–Brixton route (1870). This new form of transport, offering fares which people in all walks of life could afford, has not yet received the credit it deserves.   Ref. H/3488

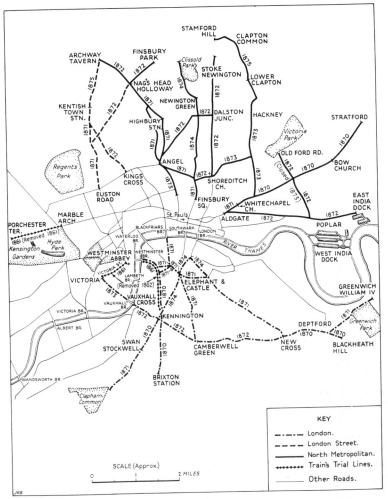

Workmen arriving in the mid-1860s by the newly introduced cheap early morning trains (right) at the Moorgate terminus of the Metropolitan Railway and (below) at Victoria (London, Chatham & Dover Railway).
Refs. U9272 and 21892

WORKMEN'S TRAINS AND TRAMS

Pearson's dream of cheap early morning trains enabling the working classes to follow the better-off into the healthier suburbs instead of being 'chained to the spot' in overcrowded dwellings in the centre, came to be realised at last when the Metropolitan Railway in May 1864 began to run two trains, one starting at 5.30 and the second at 5.40 a.m., at a threepenny return fare. By the end of 1865 between 1,800 and 2,000 workmen were using these trains every weekday, returning later by the ordinary services. In February 1865 the London, Chatham & Dover began to provide workmen's trains between its Ludgate Hill and Victoria termini round south London, one setting off from each terminus at 4.55 a.m., stopping at every station and covering the whole journey in an hour at twopence for a day return. From then onwards it became usual for any company taking property in built-up areas to provide workmen's trains in compensation. This applied to the North London Railway's Broad Street exten-sion (1865) and, in particular, to the Great Eastern's suburban lines to Edmonton and Chingford (1872 and 1873) which also put on trains at twopence return: twopenny fares were even available from Enfield Town, nearly 11 miles away. In 1884 the Great Eastern's general manager, who used to live there, commented rather haughtily on the change that had by then come over Stamford Hill, Tottenham and Edmonton:

That used to be a very nice district indeed ... with houses ... with coach houses and stables, a garden and a few acres of land. But very soon after this obligation was put upon the Great Eastern to run workmen's trains ... speculative builders went down into the neighbourhood and, as a consequence, each good house was one after another pulled down and the district given up entirely ... to the working man.

On the Great Northern line, seven workmen's trains a day were running up to London before 6.00 a.m. by the 1890s.

When the horse tramways started, the companies were obliged to provide workmen's fares at not more than a halfpenny a mile (with a penny minimum fare) and workmen's trams were run by the North Metropolitan from the outset, starting at 4.45 in the morning. The effects were the same as those of the cheap trains. 'We have relieved London of an immense number of poor people,' claimed the chairman of London Tramways Company in 1884, 'by carrying them to the suburbs. . . . Building has been going on very largely on our line of roads in south London.'

LONDONERS MOVE OUT

As London's railway and tramway systems were extended and its omnibus services improved, the number of passenger journeys grew rapidly: more than threefold in the last quarter of the nineteenth century.

More people were commuting daily to the centre of London. The City's residential population, which had already fallen from 128,000 to 75,000 between 1851 and 1871, had dropped to 27,000 by 1901. Its working population during the day, on the other hand, increased from 170,000 in 1866 to 360,000 in 1900. Similarly, the residential populations of neighbouring Westminster and Holborn fell from 340,000 to 242,000 between 1871 and 1901. By contrast, the population living within the area that eventually became that of the London County Council, encompassing Hammersmith, Hampstead, Finsbury Park, Poplar, Greenwich, Lewisham, Camberwell, Lambeth and Wandsworth, grew from 3.3 million to 4.55 million. To this needs to be added the population of outer London (the Metropolitan Police district), which

The tramways generated traffic at a remarkable rate, even though they were kept out of the central streets. The crews were smart and the horses obedient. Ref. U24982

London's rapid growth during the last 20 years of the nineteenth century.

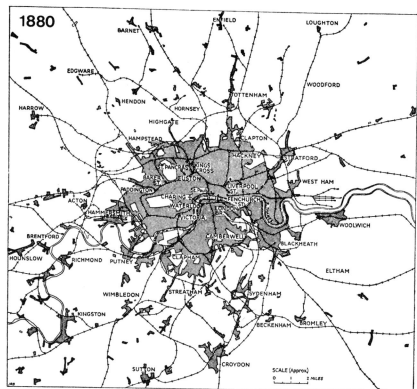

grew from 625,000 to over 2 million. All these suburbs also generated their own internal traffic.

These were years of rising purchasing power as the cost of food and raw materials fell more than earnings. The department store and high street shop attracted more customers, who often had to ride to do their shopping. Theatres and music halls gained bigger audiences; so did sporting events as Saturday half-holidays became general. All these factors contributed to the growth of off-peak as well as business travel.

The annual numbers of journeys (especially bus journeys) are difficult to calculate with accuracy, but the best

This photograph, taken at the busy Elephant and Castle junction, shows an unusual sight: a tram drawn by three mules.   Ref. H/17100

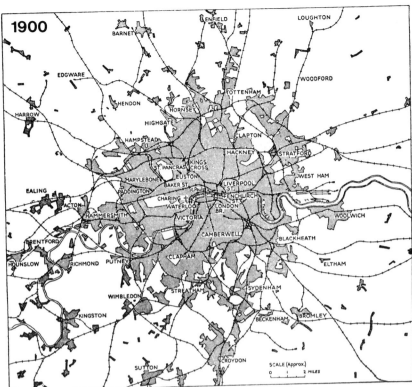

1900

SCALE (Approx.)

0   1   2 MILES

estimate suggests that those by suburban and underground train grew between 1875 and 1895 from about 150 million a year to 400 million, those by tram from 50 million to 280 million (the most impressive performance) and those by omnibus from 70 million to 300 million – an increase from 65 rides per head of Greater London's population to 165.

BETTER BUSES, BIGGER JAMS

Omnibus traffic continued to grow in the face of the new competition. Omnibuses benefited from the removal of turnpike tolls, the final abolition of mileage duty in 1870 and, in particular, the fall in fodder prices resulting from cheaper imports. They enjoyed freedom from tramway

Oxford Street in 1890: in the later nineteenth century people began to travel much more for shopping and entertainment. Ref. H/17204

In the late 19th Century congestion of horse-drawn traffic became acute in the central London streets: (above) Charing Cross in 1888, (right) London Bridge in 1897, (below) the Bank junction soon after 1900.
Refs. 24681, H/16793C and H/16871

LONDON BRIDGE. 7171. J.V.

competition in the City and West End, and they could alter their routes as required to minimise competition from tramways confined to fixed tracks.

The LGOC managed to pay its shareholders dividends of 12 per cent in some years. This encouraged competition from a rival, the London Road Car Company, using vehicles of greatly improved design. Many of their features were copied from the tramcar. Staircases to the upper deck were a considerable improvement on the insanitary vertical ladder of earlier days. The new upper-deck 'garden' seats allowed passengers to face the traffic, instead of sitting back to back as they had to do on the knifeboard buses. The Road Car

Company, which emphasised its un-French origins by flying a Union Jack at the front of all its vehicles, managed to establish itself after several years of struggle. It seems to have used tickets from the outset. The LGOC also did so, after a brief protest strike, in 1891.

Competition and lower costs caused many threepenny fares to be cut to twopence, and the number and length of penny stages to be increased. More omnibuses of improved design appeared, though the LGOC still had knifeboard seats on 40 per cent of its vehicles in 1891 – they were too old to be adapted.

The horse-drawn bus traffic reached impressive proportions by the

end of the century and provided a service frequency which modern generations may envy. During what were described as 'hours of full service', which appear to have been for most of the day, they passed through thoroughfares such as Oxford Street, Piccadilly, the Strand or Fleet Street at a rate of three or four a minute in each direction. Down Tottenham Court Road or Islington High Street they were timed at intervals of two or three per minute, and even out at Brompton Road, Praed Street or in the stretch of Edgware Road between Harrow Road and Maida Hill, one or two buses ran in each direction every minute. Somehow or other, 642 buses per hour passed along Mansion

A hansom cab outside Blackfriars station in 1906.   Ref. H/7508

(Above) The cable tramway built in 1884 up Highgate Hill was the first in Europe. Ref. 21222

(Left) In the early 1880s the LGOC's high profile encouraged a rival, the London Road Car Company, to compete with an improved type of vehicle. Ref. U12592

House Street, 606 per hour by Hyde Park Corner and 520 per hour along Whitehall. Although fares were higher than on the trams – the horse bus remained to the end a middle-class vehicle – quite long journeys could be made for relatively little. For example, a journey from Victoria to Finsbury Park (nearly seven miles) cost fourpence. This was a three-minute service and took just over the hour. The buses, though improved, were of course still basically the same small wooden vehicles as their predecessors of 50 years earlier, and could accommodate no more passengers: only about 12 inside and another 12 to 14 on top.

To this multitude of horse buses need to be added the hansom cabs and four-wheelers (11,000 of which were licensed by the police in the late 1890s) and the tradesmen's vans and carts, all horse-drawn. The traffic jams, eased by railway building in the 1860s, were again threatening the foremost city in the world with slow strangulation.

Several attempts were made to replace the slow and costly horse in urban centres. The steam engine, satisfactory for driving heavy locomotives on substantial tracks, was tried out on urban tramways. The London firm of Merryweather, already well known for its fire engines, experimented with one on Vauxhall Bridge Road as early as 1873. Other trials followed elsewhere; but in the London area steam trams were only operated commercially between Stamford Hill and Ponders End, and on a branch to Finsbury Park, between 1885 and 1890. They were not a success and the company reverted to horses.

Cable traction, powered by stationary steam engines, found favour on two London tram routes. A pioneer in the field was James Clifton Robinson, an Englishman who had been involved during the 1870s in cable tramway ventures in San Francisco using Hallidie's continuous cable system. He was also concerned with the Highgate Hill tramway, built on the Hallidie system and opened in 1884. Another cable line was opened up Brixton Hill to Streatham in December 1892, its trams being cable-hauled all the way from Kennington; it closed in 1904.

Part Two

The Electric Motor and the Internal Combustion Engine

The LGOC's B-type bus of 1910: the first really successful
mass-produced bus.
Ref. 24769

ELECTRIC TRAMWAYS

Between 1890 and 1914, particularly after 1900, two new methods of mechanical traction came to replace the horse and the steam locomotive. They greatly speeded up and cheapened passenger transport in London. For technical reasons, both had to be developed on lighter vehicles before they could be applied to heavier ones: to tramcars before trains, and to cycles and carriages ('horseless carriages') before omnibuses.

The problem of how best to transmit energy generated by steam to vehicles moving through busy streets was eventually solved in America by Frank J. Sprague. His line, built at Richmond, Virginia, in 1888, incorporated all the elements of the successful electric tram. This money-making innovation soon attracted the attention of American bankers and property speculators. In London, however, unsightly overhead wires were less readily approved; and the horse tramway companies' 21-year leases from the road authorities were due to fall in from 1891 onwards with repurchase at scrap value. It is not surprising that the electrification of London's tramways was slow to begin.

The first of them was opened by London United Tramways, a private company, on 4 April 1901: it ran from Shepherd's Bush to Acton and Kew Bridge and from Hammersmith to Kew Bridge. Extensions from Acton through Ealing and Hanwell to Southall and from Kew Bridge to Brentford and Hounslow followed on 6 July 1901. These lines were then considerably extended. Twickenham was reached in 1902,

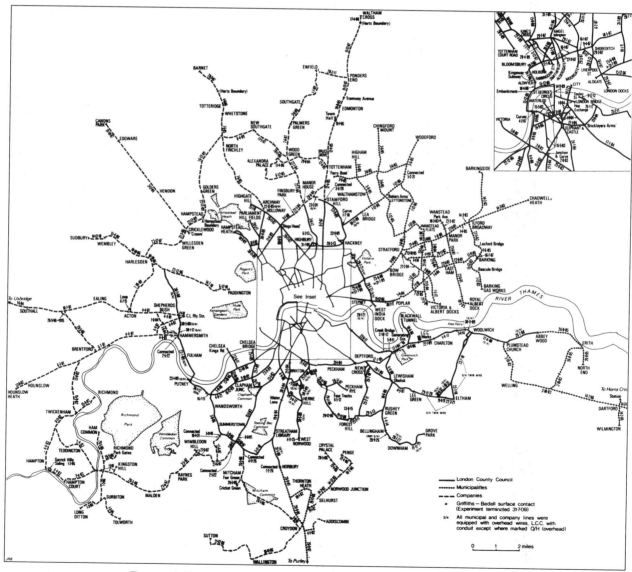

The remarkable development of electric tramways within and around London in the Edwardian years.

A London United tramcar at Shepherd's Bush on a Bank Holiday in 1903. The new electric trams were particularly busy on holidays.   Ref. 18800

Teddington, Hampton Court and Kingston Bridge in 1903, Uxbridge in 1904, Malden, Raynes Park and Wimbledon Hill in 1906–7. Metropolitan Electric Tramways developed a similarly extensive system to the north stretching out as far as Waltham Cross, and in the south the South Metropolitan system ran from Sutton, Mitcham, Crystal Palace and Penge to Croydon. Some local authorities – East and West Ham, for instance – operated their own electric tramways.

The largest and most important system of all, however, was that of the London County Council which took over, rebuilt, electrified, operated and extended the former horse tramways nearer the centre. On 15 May 1903 the first of these to be electrified was opened from Westminster and Blackfriars Bridges to Totterdown Street, Tooting, using the more expensive conduit system. LCC track was extended south of the river – and north of it too, after the LCC acquired North Metropolitan Tramways in 1906. LCC electric cars were allowed to cross Westminster Bridge and ran along the Victoria Embankment for the first time on 15 December 1906 (and across Blackfriars Bridge from 1909). The systems north and south of the river were linked for single-deck cars only by the Kingsway tunnel.

It is hard for us today to imagine the popular impact of these fine electric tramcars and the sense of pride and progress that they typified. The LCC, in particular, saw tramway electrification as an instrument of social policy, allowing poorer people to move out of the narrow, crowded streets of central London, so accelerating the movement started 40 years earlier. Its first line terminated at its housing estate at Tooting. The number of workmen's tickets, 582,000 during the last year of horse

(Above) The opening of the London County Council's first section of electric tramway, running from the southern end of Westminster Bridge to Tooting. It was an opportunity for much festivity. The Prince of Wales, accompanied by the Princess and the future Kings Edward VIII and George VI dressed in sailor suits, travelled along the route in a specially painted white tramcar festooned with evergreens. Shops closed their doors and schoolchildren were given a holiday so that they could join the cheering crowds. According to The Times, *hundreds of thousands turned out to participate in the historic occasion.* Ref. 16403

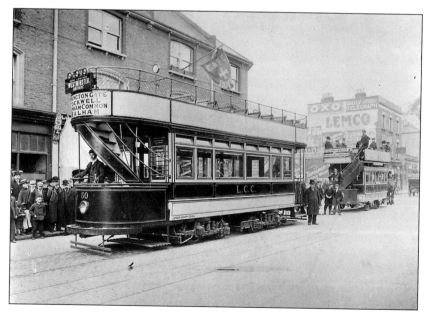

(Right) The old and the new. The LCC double-deckers, seating up to 30 passengers inside and 39 on top in the open, were far larger than the 48-seat horse trams. They were also faster and cleaner, and their fares were lower. Ref. U13111

Tramways were still forbidden in the central streets north of the river but in 1906 a tunnel was driven under the new thoroughfare, Kingsway, to enable LCC single-deckers from its northern system to reach Aldwych. It was extended to the Embankment, to link with the southern system, in 1908. (Right) A tram entering the curve from Theobald's Road; (below) the scene at the Embankment entrance. Note the conduit system between the tramlines and the absence of trolley wires. The tunnel was rebuilt in 1930–31 to accommodate double-deckers, the last of which ran through it in 1952. Part of the tunnel is now used to enable northbound road traffic coming over Waterloo Bridge to reach Kingsway without passing round the western part of Aldwych. Refs. 24765 and U27713.

trams, reached 3.34 million in the year 1906–7.

Private companies also charged lower fares and provided improved services. Passengers could ride on LUT trams for up to 3½ miles for a penny and 13 miles for fivepence. The LCC had halfpenny fares on stages half a mile long, or even more. One Edwardian observer remarked:

> *We have fast lines of electric trams, brilliantly lighted, hurrying us down from over the bridges at half the time expended under the old conditions. Each workman today in the district has had an hour added to his life – half an hour actually saved from the transit and half an hour given back to him in the transit . . . Family after family are evacuating the blocks of crowded tenements for little four-roomed cottages.*

This may have eased overcrowding and encouraged further suburban growth; it contributed little, however, to relieving congestion in the central streets from which tramways were still excluded. The electric tubes were to do this.

THE WORLD'S FIRST ELECTRIC TUBE

The advantages of driving iron cylinders through London clay had been perceived by Peter William Barlow FRS when building the piers of Lambeth Suspension Bridge. He used the technique in a horizontal direction to drive a subway seven feet in diameter and 475 yards long under the river, from Tower Hill to Pickleherring Street on the south bank. It was opened in 1870, as a little wire-hauled cable railway, but the experiment had to be discontinued after a few months; Barlow's tunnel was converted to pedestrian use, and more than a million people walked through it every year, each paying a halfpenny toll, until the opening of Tower Bridge in 1894 made it redundant.

The collapse of Barlow's experiment put an end to his bold plans to build several rail subways under London. In 1870 he had managed to get an Act passed to sanction the drilling of twin tunnels under the Thames from the Borough to King William Street; but the failure of the Tower Tunnel cable railway – not the method of its construction – made it impossible to raise the capital to finance the scheme. In 1883, however, the plan was revived by the Patent Cable Tramways Corporation, which had been set up to exploit in Britain Hallidie's endless cable system, successful in the United States and about to be demonstrated on the Highgate Hill tramway. The City of London and Southwark Subway Company was formed and obtained an Act in the following year to build a tube 1⅜ miles

long from the Elephant and Castle to the City, following – most unfortunately as it turned out – the original rapidly rising, sharply curving route from the river to its King William Street terminus at the corner of what is now called Monument Street. The company's board of directors was subsequently strengthened by several well-known City names, and chaired by a hard-headed Liverpool businessman who had been concerned, *inter alia*, with the new railway tunnelled

under the Mersey. In 1887 it secured parliamentary sanction for the railway's extension southwards from workaday Elephant and Castle to suburban Stockwell, just over three miles from the City terminus. James Henry Greathead, an able South African engineer, was appointed as engineer. He had been Barlow's assistant on the Tower Subway and had developed the special shield to drive the tunnel forwards through the London clay.

THE THAMES SUBWAY AT TOWER-HILL.

The Tower Subway: (top) the waiting room, (right) inside the subway car, which was soon discontinued. Ref. 24785

(Above) The Greathead Shield, developed for the building of the first London tube railway. The clay, when dug, was passed back through the rectangular opening. (Left) Cast iron segments were bolted in place as the shield was moved forwards. Any gaps left between the clay and the segments were then grouted (filled with liquid cement). Refs. U1097C and H/5067

Tunnelling succeeded with the new tubes as it had done with the Tower Subway, but cable traction failed again. In January 1888 the Board was informed that the Patent Cable Tramways Corporation had gone into liquidation. This was just as Sprague was about to achieve success in Virginia, and it was quickly realised that electric traction had become a feasible alternative to the mechanical cable. Electrification of the subway line was entrusted to the Manchester engineering firm of Mather & Platt, which had recently formed an electrical engineering department headed by Manchester-born Edward Hopkinson; his elder brother Dr John Hopkinson FRS, who had improved Edison's dynamo, was electrical consultant to the project. When the subway

company let the contract to Mather & Platt, therefore, they hired two men who were at the very forefront of their field.

The line was opened for traffic, and rechristened the City & South London Railway, on 18 December 1890 (several weeks after the official opening by the Prince of Wales). Unfortunately, however, this first electrically operated underground passenger railway in the world was built too small, underpowered, ill-routed (the sharp curve under the road into the single platform at the King William Street terminus was a major handicap) and not really profitable. Like many such ventures, it paid a penalty for being a pioneer, making the mistakes from which others benefited. The total passenger traffic was quite

small (a little over 5 million journeys were made in 1891) and it grew only slowly (to just under 7 million in 1899): thirty years before, the Metropolitan Railway had been handling nearly twice that amount of traffic in its early years. At a flat fare of twopence (paid at turnstiles), later increased to threepence from Stockwell in the rush hour, it was seven years before the company paid even a 2 per cent dividend. This did not encourage immediate emulation.

Parliamentary sanction was soon obtained, however, for several more tubes that were to become of importance in due course: the Central London Railway from Shepherd's Bush to the Bank (1891) and Liverpool Street (1892); the Great Northern & City from Finsbury Park to Moorgate Street; the

(Above) James Henry Greathead, who was in charge of tunnelling on the City of London & Southwark Subway (later the City & South London Railway); (below) Edward Hopkinson, its electrical engineer.
Refs. 18306 and 3278–1

(Right) The under-powered, three-carriage City & South London trains weighed only 40 tons and were hauled by tiny electric locomotives. Fluctuations in the total electrical load on the line were apt to cause the electric lights in the trains to dim to a feeble glimmer, and the company wisely decided to light its stations by gas. Each train could seat only 96 passengers, not many more than could be carried by one of the double-deck trams soon to be introduced. The little carriages were quickly nicknamed padded cells. The small frosted windows high up on each side were not intended to enable passengers to identify stations, the names of which were indicated by conductors standing on the platforms between the carriages. (Inset) The photograph of the original padded cell, with models added, was taken at the centenary exhibition held at London Transport Museum in 1990.   Refs. U32354 and 24806

Waterloo & City, from Waterloo to the Bank; the Charing Cross, Euston & Hampstead; and the Baker Street & Waterloo (all in 1893). But until more experience was gained of electric traction elsewhere, private capital was not forthcoming to build these lines.

The Central London Railway promised the best financial return, for it was

planned to run under one of London's busiest omnibus routes, via Cheapside, Holborn, Oxford Street and Bayswater Road to Shepherd's Bush. Tunnelling started in 1896 and the line to the Bank was opened officially on 27 June 1900. Samuel Clemens (Mark Twain) was present, symbolising increasing American interest, together with Sir Ernest

Cassel, Julius Wernher and their banker associates. It was the first tube to be of sufficient size and motive power to be a commercial, as distinct from a technical, success. Because of its original flat-rate fare, it came to be known as the Twopenny Tube.

The other two new tubes then to be opened had main-line railway support. The Waterloo & City (opened in 1898) enabled commuters from the London & South Western Railway to get quickly to the Bank. It was to become part of that main-line railway – and was soon known, affectionately or otherwise, as 'The Drain'. The Great Northern & City (opened in 1904) was intended to relieve the Great Northern of some of what it came to refer to as its suburban incubus. It was originally planned to carry main-line stock but did not in fact do so until recently.

In the meantime the City & South London managed to raise enough capital to by-pass its difficult curving tunnel into the King William Street terminus, by building a new line from just north of Borough station to Moorgate. This went on to the Angel, Islington, and, in the other direction, south from Stockwell to Clapham (1900). It was further extended to King's Cross and Euston in 1907.

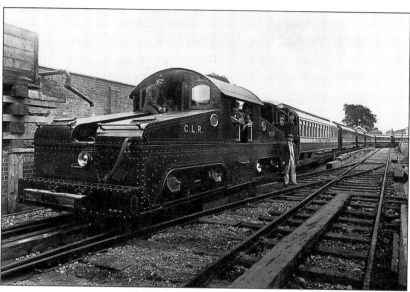

The Central London Railway was opened in 1900. It ran between Shepherd's Bush and the Bank, and avoided almost all the mistakes of the City & South London: its trains (one is shown here at the Shepherd's Bush depot) were larger, and so were its power supplies, its locomotives and the diameter of its tunnels.   Ref. U3088

But even the Central London Railway made a mistake when it used such heavy locomotives that residents above its lines complained of the vibration. Locomotives also caused reversing delays at the termini. They were replaced in 1903 by multiple-unit stock, shown here.   Ref. 24745

FINANCE FROM AMERICA

Neither the Metropolitan Railway nor the Metropolitan District Railway could stand idly by while the traffic on the steam Underground was threatened by the new deep-level tubes. By the late 1890s electric traction techniques had been developed to the point at which trains weighing 160 tons or more could be hauled by electricity. Trials were carried

Despite disappointing financial returns, the City & South London managed to raise enough capital to extend its railway south to Clapham and to build a completely new line north from Borough station to Moorgate and Islington (1900) and to Euston (1907). By 1914, when this photograph of Clapham Road (now Clapham North) station was taken, it was possible to claim quite fast journeys not only on the City & South London alone but also, by changing lines, via other tubes and the electrified Underground, to other destinations.   Ref. U12095

out by both companies in 1899 and 1900.

The Central London Railway's success led to a flood of Bills in the 1901 session – so many, in fact, that a parliamentary Joint Select Committee was formed to adjudicate among them.

By then there had appeared on the scene an American with a uniquely extensive knowledge of urban transport electrification and its financing. This was the flamboyant Charles Tyson Yerkes, a wheeler-dealer (the model for Charles Algernon Cowperwood, 'The Titan' of Theodore Dreiser's trilogy), who had made a fortune from Chicago's rapid

transit system by various devious and often corrupt methods before the city fathers decided he could bribe them no longer. In England Yerkes's more dubious business habits were restrained by close association with a leading Methodist, Sir Robert William Perks MP, who had been solicitor to the Metropolitan Railway and was well versed in the art of British company promotion. His financial adviser was Edgar Speyer, head of a London merchant bank with offices in New York and Frankfurt.

With so much practical experience of lucrative tramway and local railway promotions in the United States, Yerkes

could not resist seizing the opportunities offered by electrification possibilities in London, where so many railways had already been sanctioned by Parliament and only awaited finance. In London, living with his wife and mistress (and carrying on various affairs on the side, though he was now in his 60s), this energetic elderly capitalist was clearly in his element.

He realised at the outset that substantial profits could be produced by property development if the proposed Hampstead tube were to be extended beyond its authorised limits, beyond Kentish Town to the Archway Tavern at

Our Engineers are now engaged upon the Preliminary Work in connection with the Construction of **UNDERGROUND ELECTRIC RAILWAYS** in London, and their special experience in this department will be of immense value in obtaining Electric Railway Contracts.

POPULARITY OF THE NEW UNDERGROUND.

London's latest novelty and its advantages.

"No fewer than 84,500 passengers had sampled the new line on its opening day. Thousands more had looked on.

"As the line is open seven days a week, these numbers, if regarded as average traffic figures, would mean a yearly passenger return of 30,000,000."

DAILY MAIL, August 1st, 1900.

"Meantime London, all agape, crowds to the Twopenny Tube. Thursday's traffic returns completely eclipse the previous days, as the following list shows :—

Monday	83,000	passengers.
Tuesday	91,600	passengers.
Wednesday	86,000	passengers.
Thursday	93,000	passengers.

"Yesterday the crowds swayed and surged to get on to the trains. It was a cosmopolitan throng. Nearly every civilised nation under the sun was represented among the humanity that was struggling to experience London's latest sensation."

DAILY MAIL, August 4th, 1900.

"When a place is Royally opened it is not always really opened. A week or two back the Prince of Wales inaugurated the Central London Railway, but not till yesterday was it available to the public. Not till yesterday, therefore, could expectation be confirmed by experience. It was. The railway is a valuable acquisition to London."

DAILY NEWS, July 31st, 1900.

(Above) Promoters of other tube companies used an artist to emphasise the Central London's success in order to whip up financial support for their own ventures.
Ref. U34633

(Right) Charles Tyson Yerkes, benefactor of London: he managed to persuade his fellow-Americans that fortunes were to be made out of London tubes.   Ref. 11628

(Above) Ripe for development: Golders
Green, looking north up Finchley Road with
North End Road branching off on the right.
This photograph was taken in 1906, just
before the line was opened. Carriages had
already arrived and can be seen in the siding
behind the tree on the right.   Ref. 24783

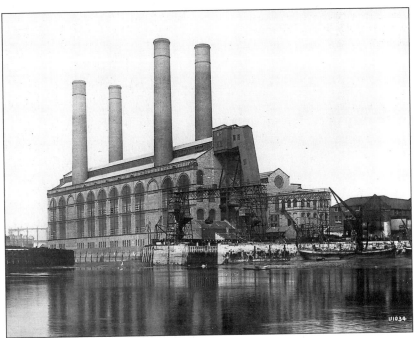

(Right) Underground Electric Railways' vast
power station, built at Lots Road in Chelsea
between 1902 and 1904.   Ref. U1034

Highgate and under the Heath to an open-air terminus at Golders Green, described at the time by a parliamentary witness as 'absolutely open country, for the simple reason that there is no means of getting to it'. The Metropolitan District, electrification of which had first drawn Yerkes's attention to London's possibilities, owned the rights to build a tube from South Kensington to Piccadilly. This attracted his interest to that tube, too, with a view to its extension to Finsbury Park, taking advantage of another tube scheme that had already been authorised. He also added to his collection the Baker Street & Waterloo Railway, the building of which had halted abruptly after its chief backer, Whitaker Wright's London & Globe Finance Corporation, had gone into liquidation in December 1900. Rivalry from another rough diamond, the equally unscrupulous American J Pierpont Morgan, was checked by Yerkes's acquisition of the new, electrified and rapidly expanding London United Tramways. He created, in 1902, the Underground Electric Railways Company of London Ltd, with a capital of £5 million in half a million £10 shares. The new company had three aims: to acquire the Metropolitan District Electric Traction Company, formed the previous year, to finance the three tube undertakings, and to build a large power station at Lots Road, Chelsea, an ideal site for the supply of coal by river. Most of Yerkes's financial support came from institutions and individuals in the United States who, no doubt, remembered the profits he had managed to make in Chicago. British investors were much more cautious: they had a closer knowledge of the costs involved, and thus of the higher risks.

The three tubes were separately promoted at first (they were brought

Trial trip of a new electric train before it went into regular service on the Metropolitan Railway's main line out of Baker Street in early January 1905. Stock of the sort used here by the District Railway was employed on the Circle, which was electrified with delay and difficulty later the same year. Refs. U37863 and H/6952

together in 1910 as the London Electric Railway Company). Yerkes soon ran into difficulty in raising the capital needed for their construction and resorted to the ingenious device of offering to existing UERL shareholders 5 per cent profit-sharing notes at 96, redeemable at par on or before 1 June 1908 – by which time, he confidently expected, some profits would be available for distribution. This new paper proved attractive; about half of it ($16.5 million worth) was taken up in America. Later, when even more capital was required, 4 per cent debentures were issued, secured by mortgage of the power station and tubes already partly built. These, together with UERL's original £5 million and the £7 million raised by the profit-sharing notes, brought the total raised by Yerkes and his friends to £15 million.

The Metropolitan Railway, in the meantime much stronger financially, had been able to raise about £1.5 million to electrify its Aldgate–South Kensington section of the Circle and, with its own power station at Neasden, its line out from Baker Street. Metropolitan electric trains began to run from Baker Street to Harrow and Uxbridge on 1 January 1905.

The Metropolitan District Railway brought over a team of engineers from America and experimented with electrification in 1903 on an extension, as yet unopened to traffic, between Ealing and South Harrow. It ordered equipment from British Thomson Houston (BTH), the British subsidiary of General Electric of America. Electric trains started regular service between South Acton and Hounslow Barracks (Hounslow West) on 13 June 1905, and on the main line between Ealing and Whitechapel on 1 July 1905. Attempts by the two underground companies to operate the Circle electrically started on the same day, but there were teething troubles and a reliable, regular service was not possible until 24 September.

The three UERL tubes, built astonishingly quickly, followed soon after: from Baker Street to Elephant and Castle in 1906 (extended to Edgware Road in 1907), from Finsbury Park to Hammersmith at the end of 1906, and from Charing Cross to Golders Green and Highgate (Archway) in the middle of 1907. Together with the Central

Line, the three other tubes and the old underground, newly electrified and capable of carrying more trains per hour, they added greatly to passenger transport capacity in the centre and helped to relieve some of the road congestion. The London travelling public were the immediate gainers. Unfortunately for the UERL's shareholders, however, traffic did not begin to reach Yerkes's optimistic forecasts. But by then he had left the scene. He died at the Waldorf-Astoria Hotel in New York (not at his home in the city, with his wife) on 29 December 1905 at the age of 68.

MOTOR BUSES

The successful mechanisation of London's omnibuses was soon to supplement all this additional carrying capacity. Experiments had been carried out in London with battery electric and steam vehicles during the 1890s and with petrol engines from the beginning of the new century. There were many attempts to develop regular services before the technology had been adequately developed and become capable of withstanding the constant starting and stopping in heavy traffic. During 1905 hundreds of thousands of pounds were raised by several companies whose vehicles, adequate while new, soon began breaking down with the rigours of everyday use. Horse omnibuses could still compete. The LGOC wisely held back, merely trying out a few motor buses here and there. In February 1907 it hired Frank Searle, a locomotive engineer by training who had gained motor experience with a rival concern, and soon appointed him its chief motor engineer.

Fierce competition in the London bus business enabled the prudent LGOC to acquire its enfeebled, broken-down rival the Road Car Company, which had

This curiously ugly Road Car steam bus – clearly an adaptation of a horse bus body stretched on top to carry 36 passengers – started to run on 17 March 1902. It made a special point of serving the new terminus of the Central London Railway at Shepherd's Bush. It was withdrawn from service after two months, however. Later trials had a little more success and Thomas Clarkson's National steam buses, operating in London in small numbers from 1909, did much better during wartime but were withdrawn in 1919. Battery-driven electric vehicles never got beyond the experimental stage. Ref. 18724

The first reliable and commercially successful petrol buses in London: (below) an early LGOC X-type taking a party of children on an outing, and (bottom) its successor and the real winner, the B-type, in general service. Both were produced at Walthamstow works under Frank Searle's direction, the X-type in 1909 and the B-type from 1910. Note the bus crews' new jackets and caps.   Refs. U9189 and H/13579

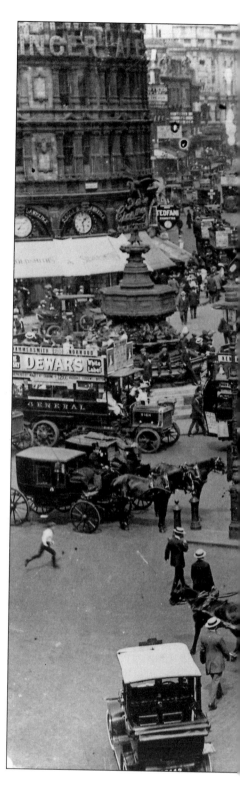

By 1912 motor buses dominated the scene in Piccadilly Circus, among them a white National steam bus. Motor taxis were also plentiful, but some hackneys and all goods vehicles were still horse-drawn. In this photograph the traffic discipline seems poor, and the pedestrians include some rather reckless jay-walkers.   Ref. 20063

moved too fast into untried motors. The Vanguard Company, the largest of the newcomers, was another LGOC victim. It was at the Vanguard's small overhaul works at Walthamstow that Searle designed and built the first really promising motor bus, the X-type, which took to the streets on 12 August 1909. An improved version, the B-type, was on the road in October 1910, the conductors and drivers being at last given uniform jackets and caps to mark the event. The Walthamstow works was extended in 1909, and was soon employing more than a thousand men and producing 20 vehicles per week. The LGOC was able to take its last horse omnibus out of service at the end of October 1911, although some other operators continued to run them for a little longer.

Each new motor bus was cheaper to operate than its horse-drawn predecessor and could earn more. It carried 50 per cent more passengers (16 inside and 18 on top) at twice the average speed even when limited by the law, and therefore by timetabling, to 12 m.p.h. Motor buses, running on public roads, were soon very profitable, while the newly electrified Underground was struggling to make itself pay at all.

THE UERL AND LGOC MERGER

When it was clear that the electrified Underground and the tubes were not generating the additional traffic forecast by their optimistic promoters, the UERL's American shareholders sent over their own troubleshooter. On 20 February 1907 they appointed as general manager, at the impressive salary of £2,000 a year, a young American tramway expert. This dynamo of a man was Albert Henry Stanley, the future Lord Ashfield, then aged 32. Though he

Thomas Tilling was the main independent company, though it ran as an associate of the LGOC. The company owned many horse buses; the top one was photographed in 1903. It also experimented with Milnes–Daimler petrol vehicles – the one above was photographed in the company garage in 1905 – but concentrated eventually on a fleet of Tilling–Stevens petrol-electrics, which began running in 1911. The last horse bus to run in service in London was one of Tilling's; it ran from Peckham Rye to Honor Oak tavern on 4 August 1914 – the day the First World War broke out.   Refs. 19009 and U28590

came on a three-year contract, he was to dominate London's transport for the next forty years. He joined George Stegmann Gibb, who had been recruited (we would say head-hunted) as manag-

ing director by Yerkes's successor as chairman, Edgar Speyer, from the North Eastern Railway where he had already gained a reputation as one of the country's outstanding authorities on the collection and use of railway statistics. Gibb had taken office on 1 January 1906 and, in his turn, had brought down from York a younger colleague, Frank Pick, also to be intimately associated with London Transport's later successes.

The new team made every effort to increase revenue. Through booking was introduced on the District Railway, the three tubes and London United Tramways. Walter Gott, a Yorkshireman with a real flair for publicity, produced the

Albert Stanley in 1910.   Ref. H/16473

company's first maps, folders and posters. Fares were raised for longer journeys, where electric railways had a speed advantage over other forms of transport. The frequency of service was greatly improved by the use of automatic signalling: rush-hour frequency from South Kensington was increased from 24 trains an hour to 30 in February 1908 and to 40 from December 1911. The time of the journey from Ealing to Mansion House was reduced from 48 minutes by steam to 32, that from Hounslow from 60 to 47 and that from Wimbledon from 45 to 34. Discounted strip tickets were sold on the three tubes.

A UERL poster of 1908, extolling the delights of Golders Green (and Hendon and Finchley beyond).   Ref. 10705

Somehow UERL's enterprising management clawed its way back to solvency. In 1908 the working losses after payment of debt charges at last turned to gain. The profit-sharing notes were renegotiated at the very last moment, on 30 June that year, although it was touch and go. Receipts from the Metropolitan District rose from £488,000 in 1906 to £691,000 in 1910, by which time the three tubes were earning even more, £729,000.

Gibb left UERL in April 1910 to become chairman of the government's

*By 1914 the Combine was issuing posters for
special events, such as an early air show at
Hendon.*   Ref. U45859

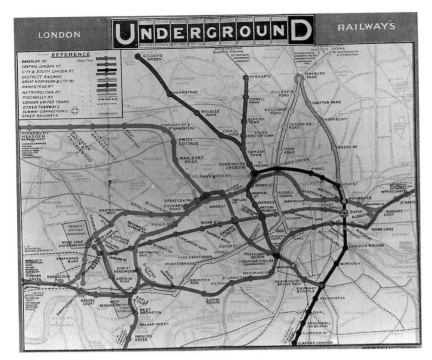

(Left) A very early (1908) version of the Underground map. (Below) Harry Beck, a specialist in electric circuit diagrams who was then on contract to the Combine, produced the first diagrammatic plan as a speculative venture in 1931. The management of the Underground was doubtful at first, but was persuaded to publish. The map subsequently became, in its many updated and revised versions, an international design classic.   Refs. H/16428 and 13946

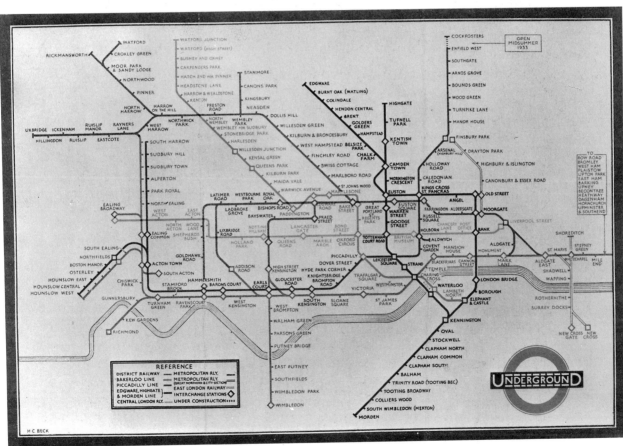

newly formed Road Board. The Americans' nominee general manager, Albert Stanley, who had been made a director in 1908, succeeded him as managing director. He was not yet 36.

In 1910, with its new motor buses, the LGOC threatened to become a serious competitor to the Underground, and it was certainly becoming financially stronger. Its profits in the year ended September 1911 totalled £214,000, nearly £100,000 more than the year

tion from the new (though soon to be defunct) motor bus rivals and had now recovered, thanks to the B-type bus, to £200. But such a high figure could not possibly be maintained if Daimler competition were to materialise. By early February 1912 most LGOC shareholders had accepted the UERL offer and the LGOC Board was soon reconstituted, with Stanley and other UERL men in a majority. The Walthamstow bus works was turned into a wholly

UERL tramway, the LUT. When 225 Daimlers came on the road at the end of January 1913, they did not fight what was already being called the Combine but ran in friendly association with it.

MET was followed by two other companies. The Central London Railway had been extended from Shepherd's Bush to the Franco-British Exhibition site at Wood Lane (White City) in 1908 and from the Bank to Liverpool Street in 1912. Both the Central London and the City & South London were then losing traffic to the buses or the electric trams. Within a few months both accepted attractive offers from the UERL.

After 1913 only the Metropolitan Railway (and the Great Northern & City which it acquired in 1913), the LCC tramway network and the local services of the main-line companies lay outside the Combine's control. The UERL, which had been on the verge of collapse when the profit-sharing notes fell due in 1908, had contrived to manoeuvre itself into a very strong position indeed. The managing director had achieved great things in five years and well deserved the knighthood which he was to receive in 1914 in recognition of his services to London's transport.

Even before 1914 London was a popular tourist destination for Americans, despite the fact that the pound was strong. Twice a week, Motor Jobmasters ran morning and afternoon sightseeing tours from Paddington station. The speed limit of 12 miles per hour applied to all such vehicles at that time. So did the solid rubber tyres.   Ref. H/16870C

before. Now, however, this rosy outlook was threatened by a vehicle manufacturer: Daimler, part of the powerful Birmingham Small Arms Company, objected to the LGOC's making its own vehicles rather than purchasing them from outside.

Stanley, with Speyer's help, seized his opportunity. At the end of December 1911 he made the LGOC an offer in UERL 6 per cent first cumulative preference and other shares that it could not refuse. Contemporaries valued the package as worth £227 for each LGOC £100 share. Yet these, not long before, had been forced down to £17 by competi-

owned subsidiary, Associated Equipment Co. (AEC).

Another transport undertaking now succumbed. This was the Metropolitan Electric Tramways, a subsidiary of the powerful British Electric Traction Company. Fearing that it would lose traffic from the north London tube stations when they came to be served by LGOC buses, it had countered by setting up its own bus operating subsidiary, run by Daimlers. Now it came to terms. A holding company, London and Suburban Traction Ltd, was formed to acquire the share capital of the MET, the MET's new bus subsidiary and the

MAIN-LINE DEVELOPMENTS

The electric tramways, electric railways and motor buses deprived the main lines, including the London & North Western's protégé the North London Railway, of much of their local traffic. They responded in kind to the new competition. Additional tracks were built into some of the main termini, two of which (Victoria and Waterloo) were considerably enlarged. From 1906 Great Central trains from

(Above) 'Down stairs' from the District Railway to the tubes at Charing Cross (now Embankment) in 1921, but (right) signs direct passengers to the 'moving stairway' at Earl's Court, the first in continuous use on the system. Already in place were the helpful indicators that lit up to show the order in which trains would arrive; they remained in use until very recently. Refs. U617 and U10188

Marylebone began to run local services (along with the Metropolitan) to such agreeable, lush and leafy locations as Pinner, Northwood, Rickmansworth, Chorleywood, Amersham, Great Missenden and Wendover. The Great Northern's Enfield branch was extended to Cuffley. More passengers came in on main-line suburban trains from outer London, where the population was growing most rapidly.

Nearer the centre, those main-line companies that could afford it turned to electrification. Electric trains began to run regularly on the London, Brighton & South Coast Railway's South London Loop (London Bridge to Victoria via Peckham Rye and Brixton) from 1 December 1909. The system was extended to Crystal Palace via Streatham Hill (1911) and from Peckham Rye Junction (1912). The London & South Western Railway began to run some

Main-line responses to greater competition: (right) a London, Brighton & South Coast Railway train, which used the single-phase a.c. overhead wire system, at Wandsworth Road in about 1915; (below) a London & South Western Railway train, using the third-rail 660-volt d.c. system which was later adopted generally by the Southern Railway, on the East Putney–Wimbledon line in or after 1916.

suburban electric trains from Waterloo from October 1915. By 1916 the fastest trains reached Putney in 12 minutes instead of 20 minutes by steam, Richmond in 22 minutes instead of 34 and Twickenham in 27 minutes instead of 41. These marked the beginnings of main-line electrification south of the river, which was to be vastly extended between the wars.

North of the river, Bakerloo tube trains reached Queen's Park in 1915, Willesden Junction later that year and Watford in 1917. North London electric trains began running from Broad Street to Richmond in October 1916. The Great Eastern Railway could not afford electrification, but regained traffic by running many more steam trains and by cutting fares.

SECOND TO NONE

With all this new public transport provision in the last years of the Long Peace, London was universally admired by visitors and transport specialists from all over the world. Under the Combine, and with Frank Pick in charge of a Traffic Development and Advertising Department from April 1912, it was the turn of the bus services to be greatly improved and extended. They no longer started at middle-class hours or charged middle-class fares, and the distance covered by the LGOC and its associates increased from 195 million miles in 1912 to 528 million in 1914. In the centre, buses ran about every 15 seconds in each direction, even between seven and eight o'clock in the evening,

past the Ritz Hotel in Piccadilly and through Oxford Street just to the west of Oxford Circus. Routes were extended up to 15 miles or more, often more than twice the distance covered by horse omnibuses. More services radiated from central railway termini (40 instead of 12 from Victoria, for instance) and there was particular scope for buses serving stations farther out. In 1911 the perimeter of motor bus services was described by a line drawn through Hendon, Dollis Hill, Finsbury Park, Walthamstow, Wanstead, Ilford, Sidcup, Bromley, Dulwich, Barnes, Chiswick, Ealing and Willesden. By 1914 daily motor services were stretching from Golders Green to St Albans, Stockwell to Reigate, Peckham to Hounslow and Twickenham to Highgate. On Sundays

A Bakerloo train at Willesden Junction in 1917. Each carriage still had its own guard; at that stage of the war most of the guards were women.   Ref. 4262–1

THE OPEN ROAD
FRESH AIR AND SUNSHINE

Just before the outbreak of war in 1914, when this poster was issued, the Combine was encouraging Londoners to take its motor buses into the country. Longer routes were covered on Sundays and public holidays.   Ref. 24790

they ran even farther afield: from Clapham Common to Dorking (nearly 21 miles), from Hounslow to Maidenhead (nearly 20 miles), from Ealing to Leatherhead, and from Liverpool Street to Hampton Court.

By this time most passenger vehicles in central London were motorised (including motor taxi cabs, introduced in 1907 and increasing to a total of nearly 8,400 of the 10,000 or so cabs remaining in 1913). A traffic census conducted in 1911 showed that only 13 per cent of all passenger vehicles in the London area were still horse-drawn. In 1913 this figure had fallen to 6 per cent (although, by contrast, 88 per cent of goods vehicles were still being drawn by horses).

The years between 1896 and 1913 thus saw a great extension and speeding up of London's passenger transport services. The number of journeys by train made each year had increased from about 400 million to 710 million; those by bus and tram, though shorter, had shot up from 600 million to about 1,545 million. The number of journeys made each year by the average resident of Greater London grew from 165 to just over 300 in those 17 years. Clearly, this was a period of immense significance. London has certainly seen nothing comparable since.

Part Three

The Years of
Ashfield and Pick

The new UERL headquarters at 55 Broadway.
Ref. 24371

THE FIRST WORLD WAR

Some motor buses were commandeered at the outbreak of war, and hundreds more were soon required. Some went to Belgium and France, many of them to the battle areas. One driver personally captured 12 Germans near Armentières and drove back with them on the top deck. Bus B43, named 'Old Bill' after the war, was involved at Antwerp, Ypres, the Somme and elsewhere. Others found their way to the Rhine after the Armistice.

Older vehicles, some of them horse drawn, had to be recalled for service on the London streets to carry not only regular passengers but also many munition workers and servicemen passing through London or on leave. Police regulations were relaxed to allow passengers to stand inside for the first time. The tramways and railways had also to handle much additional traffic. As more transport men went into the forces, their places were taken by women, many of them formerly domestic servants.

The UERL's bus manufacturing subsidiary, AEC, produced over ten thousand three- and four-ton trucks, 40 per cent of the total supplied to the forces. This feat was achieved by moving-line production, the earliest British example in the motor industry.

Damage from bombing was small compared with the destruction in and after 1940. In the 12 raids on the London area by airship and 19 by plane, only two buses and a tram were wrecked. One tram depot was hit.

In 1915 the Underground Group set up a Common Fund into which the various constituent companies apart from LUT paid their surpluses after working expenses, interest and dividends on prior stocks had been deducted. This saved inter-company accounting and indicated the relative profitability of the various concerns at the time: LGOC 40%; LER (the three tubes) 26%; CLR 20%; MDR 12%; and C&SLR 2%. The Combine's takeover of the LGOC and the CLR had evidently been very advantageous indeed.

British troops and a Metropolitan Tramways B-type bus at Ostend.   Ref. 24768

(Right) A woman bus conductor in wartime . . .   Ref. 14612

. . . and (below) women working in the LGOC's engineering shop.   Ref. 24777

INTO PUBLIC CONTROL

The prewar mergers of 1912–13 clearly pointed the way ahead. A traffic authority for the whole of London was recommended immediately after the war, when fare levels were being discussed, and again when the allocation of government funds under the Trade Facilities Act (1921) was under consideration a few years later. The London and Home Counties Advisory Committee, formed under the provisions of the London Traffic Act (1924), drew the Minister of Transport's attention to the 'acute and wasteful competition' between the various transport concerns operating over the whole area from St Albans to Dorking and from Slough to Gravesend. Bidden by the

electric tramways were already under pressure from the improved and more flexible motor buses, and the Combine each promoted a Co-ordination of Passenger Transport Bill in the 1928–29 session of Parliament. They both passed the Commons; almost immediately, however, Parliament was dissolved and a Labour government was returned, with Herbert Morrison as the new Minister of Transport.

The two Bills were dropped. But Morrison and Ashfield, despite their different political outlooks, collaborated to produce a solution which remained generally acceptable even after the Labour government fell in 1931. The London Passenger Transport Board was to be a public corporation along the lines of the Conservative-inspired Central

Frank Pick, a Lincolnshire draper's son, shunned the limelight and never secured public honours.

Pick, who paid immense attention to detail at headquarters and in his regular inspection trips around the Underground, was the ideal complement to Ashfield. Born at Spalding on 23 November 1878, he won a scholarship to St Peter's School, York, and went on to take a London degree in law. In 1902, at the age of 23, he started work for the North Eastern Railway which, with Gibb as general manager, was pioneering modern management methods among British railway companies. Gibb brought him to London in 1906 and he moved rapidly up the UERL management ladder, becoming traffic officer in 1909 and commercial manager in 1912 at the age of 34. Stanley recognised his qualities and was responsible for putting him in charge of a department at the Board of Trade in 1917. In 1921 he became UERL joint assistant managing director and in 1928 managing director. He worked ferociously hard, keeping two secretaries ceaselessly at work typing memoranda and answers to correspondence. He was interested in the visual arts and paid equal attention to the design of a teacup as to that of a new suburban station – his name has come to be particularly closely associated with the forward-looking architectural merits of the stations built between the wars. In 1928 he became president of the Design and Industries Association, and in 1934 was appointed the first chairman of the Council for Art and Industry.
Ref. 20091

The Combine informs the public of the resources needed to run its bus and Underground services in 1923.   Refs. 24791 and 24792

Minister of Transport to prescribe a remedy, the Advisory Committee recommended an extension of the UERL's Common Fund with common management.

The Metropolitan Railway would not participate; but the LCC, whose

Electricity Board (set up in 1926) and the British Broadcasting Corporation (1927). It was to consist of a chairman, vice-chairman and five (later seven) members, chosen for their ability and experience not by the Minister but by five independent appointing trustees (the chairman of the LCC, a representative of the London and Home Counties Traffic Advisory Committee, the chairman of Committee of London Clearing Bankers and the Presidents of the Institute of Chartered Accountants and the Law Society). Shareholders in UERL and the Metropolitan Railway were to be issued with various transport stocks, and the independent companies were compensated with either stocks or cash. The LCC, Middlesex and Hertfordshire County Councils' and West Ham County Borough received stock. The other interested local authorities got cash, in two cases with some stock as well. The new undertaking was to be run as a business, free from political interference.

Ashfield used his powerful influence to persuade his shareholders to agree to the financial arrangements. The four main-line companies agreed to a pool for all traffic in the London area, the proportions in which provide the best pointer towards the relative strengths of the new LPTB and the London suburban services of the main lines: LPTB 62 per cent and main lines 38 per cent, of which the lion's share, 25 per cent, went to the Southern Railway. There was no common management, but a Joint Standing Committee was set up; this meant that representatives of the LPTB and the main lines met regularly to discuss matters of common interest.

The LPTB took over on 1 July 1933; only Tillings and a few other bus operators then preferred to stay outside. Ashfield had achieved almost all his objectives and continuity was maintained. He remained chairman in the fine new headquarters which UERL had opened in 1930. Pick, managing director from 1928, continued in that position and became vice-chairman.

From odd job man on the Detroit tramways to a pillar of the British Establishment: Albert Henry Stanley, Baron Ashfield of Southwell, photographed here with his daughter at the opening of the reconstructed City & South London Railway in 1924.

His father, Henry Knattries, married a girl from Derby and he himself was born there on 8 August 1874. The family emigrated to America, where Knattries changed his surname to Stanley and was employed as a coachbuilder in Detroit. Albert went to work for Detroit Street Railways, having secured – and no doubt continued to secure in the evenings – an education at 'various American colleges and technical schools'. He displayed management flair and rose to become general superintendent at the age of 28. In the following year he moved to the Street Railway Department of the Public Service Corporation of New Jersey, where he became superintendent in 1904 and general manager in 1907. Sent to London soon after by the American shareholders of UERL (page 69), he brought the business together and saved it from disaster, became managing director in 1910 and then with the chairman, the merchant banker Edgar Speyer, acquired the London General Omnibus Company, the Central London Railway and other transport undertakings. At that time he was very much a working manager, driving himself and everyone else to greater efforts. He was knighted in 1914.

He was brought into Lloyd George's first government in December 1916 as President of the Board of Trade, taking his seat in Parliament as Member for Ashton-under-Lyne (his friend Max Aitken resigned in his favour and went to the Lords as Baron Beaverbrook). He left the Government in 1919, returning to UERL as its chairman as well as managing director, and was created Baron Ashfield in 1920. His function thereafter was to mingle with the good and the great (by common consent he had immense charm) in order to secure public guarantees for the further private capital needed for the extensions to the Underground. He was also in demand to serve on the boards of other big businesses: he was a director of the Midland Bank and, as chairman of the British Dyestuffs Corporation, he was involved in the creation of ICI, which he also served as a director.   Ref. 17099

It was a fortunate accident when Herbert Morrison, photographed here in 1929, became Labour Minister of Transport. He had a particular interest in London and was prepared to collaborate with Ashfield in creating what was to become the London Passenger Transport Board.   Ref. H/16446

THE SPREAD OF ELECTRIFICATION

Having outlined the final stages in the creation of what was to become known as London Transport, we now retrace our steps and look at the very considerable progress achieved in the development of rail and road transport during those economically troubled years before 1933.

After the First World War the main-line suburban services offered the most scope for electrification. It was pursued most actively south of London by Sir Herbert Walker, already concerned with earlier electrification out of Waterloo, when he took charge of the Southern Railway. He established an electrical department in 1923 and started a rolling programme for the electrification of Southern's remaining suburban lines, totalling 264 route miles and eventually costing £11.5 million.

This was completed on 6 July 1930. In the process, the overhead wires were replaced by a third rail system.

The Underground's major extension of the 1920s involved penetration into the Southern's territory: on 13 September 1926 the City & South London was extended from Clapham Common to Morden, where a bus station was provided. This was part of what came to be known as the Northern Line. Taking advantage of the Trade Facilities Act (1921), which was essentially a job-creation measure whereby the Treasury guaranteed the interest on capital borrowed for new works until those ventures could pay their way, the UERL had already set about extending its line north from Golders Green to Hendon Central (opened 19 November 1923) and Edgware (18 August 1924). The link between Euston and Camden Town was opened on 20 April 1924, and that from Strand to Kennington on

13 September 1926. All the old C&SL tunnels had to be enlarged to the standard width, a complex process which involved restricting services and closing the line for a time. The Euston–Moorgate section was reopened for traffic on 20 April 1924 and Moorgate–Clapham Common the following 1 December.

North of the river, main-line electrification had started before the war. Now it was continued. Full electric train services started to run out of Euston on 10 July 1922. The Croxley Green branch was opened on 30 October 1922 and that to Rickmansworth on 26 September 1927. But the electrification of the Southend line, which the LMS had inherited, proceeded slowly: District trains did not run over its electrified track from Barking to Upminster until 12 September 1932. Out of Liverpool Street the Great Eastern, and its successor the LNER, continued the policy of

Lord Ashfield (seated centre) and his first London Passenger Transport Board in July 1933. Seated on the left is Sir John Gilbert, chairman of the LCC 1920–21, and on the right Sir Henry Maybury, the highway engineer and authority on roads and road transport. Standing, from left to right: John Cliff, assistant general secretary of the Transport and General Workers Union, Patrick Ashley Cooper, governor of the Hudson's Bay Company, Frank Pick and Sir Edward Holland, chairman of Surrey County Council 1926–30.

Charles Holden's new UERL headquarters at 55 Broadway was opened in 1930 above St James's Park station. Thirteen floors high (the top four floors were not used until after the Second World War because of fire regulations), the building was so arranged that there was daylight in every office. On the exterior Jacob Epstein carved a pair of groups, 'Day' and 'Night' (inset depicts 'Night'), directly from the stone in situ on the building. 55 Broadway, near Parliament and Buckingham Palace, became a worthy physical tribute to London Transport's status in its prime. It attracted talented staff who wanted to work there, and were proud to do so. Refs. U6170 and U5520

operating more steam trains – from July 1920 it provided the most intensive steam train service in the world.

The Metropolitan Railway extended its electric trains from Harrow to Rickmansworth on 5 January 1925 and opened the branch to Watford on 2 November 1926. The FA Cup Final began to be played at Wembley in 1923, and the British Empire Exhibition was staged there in 1924 and again in 1925. Both events generated considerable traffic at certain times. More people went to live in Metroland, which was enlarged when the Stanmore Line was opened from Wembley Park on 10 December 1932. In the centre, the Metropolitan electrified its widened lines east of King's Cross to allow more trains to Moorgate Street at peak times. In 1929 it also greatly changed the outward appearance of its main terminus at Baker Street by building over it an impressive block of flats, known as Chiltern Court.

The Underground Group was also busy with other extensions north of the river. The Central London's prewar scheme to build a half-mile extension from Wood Lane to join a railway to Ealing, to be built by the Great Western Railway, was soon completed. CLR trains ran over it to Ealing Broadway from 3 August 1920.

At the end of the 1920s, UERL took advantage of another job creation measure, the Labour government's Development (Loan Guarantees and Grants) Act (1929). The Piccadilly Line was extended a further 7¾ miles to Cockfosters. Opened in stages from September 1932, the railway was completed through to the new terminus on 31 July 1933. It was also extended westwards over existing tracks from Hammersmith to Acton, South Harrow, Rayners Lane and Uxbridge (opened throughout on 23 October 1933) and to Hounslow West (13 March 1933).

Pick's friend, the gifted Lancashire-born architect, Charles Holden, had undertaken station and other work for the Combine, starting with the façade of Bond Street Station (1924); but it was

Ealing Broadway in 1933, 13 years after the start of the Central London Railway service there.
Ref. H/17306

Croxley Green station in 1936, 14 years after the arrival of the first electric trains.   Ref. U19603

Idyllic Metroland as depicted in a Metropolitan Railway brochure.
Ref. H/16403

(Above) In 1923 the station forecourt at Golders Green, when the railway was being extended northwards, was still fairly peaceful; (left) nor was the exit from Edgware station exactly congested when a train had just arrived there in 1927, three years after that branch had reached its northern terminus.   Refs. U2308 and U4116

Escalators nearing completion at Bank station in 1924.   Ref. U2577

Two impressive Piccadilly Line stations designed by Charles Holden: (middle) the booking hall at Southgate, (bottom) platforms at Cockfosters.   Refs. H/16303 and U15823

for these Piccadilly extensions in particular that he produced his most attractive, highly functional designs. No less important for the travelling public were the fine new stations built in central London to replace the rather cramped originals. Oxford Circus, Bank, Tottenham Court Road and Piccadilly Circus – the last the most impressive of all – were among the 35 stations modernised throughout the system during the 1920s. A further 16 were 'improved'.

LARGER BUSES CARRY MORE PASSENGERS

Despite the rapid success of the AEC motor bus before the war, further development enabled more passengers – 46 or more instead of 34 – to be carried at almost the same cost. This was good for the LGOC; but the more lucrative the industry, the more attractive it became for competitors too.

Bus design steadily improved, although the Metropolitan Police would not allow experiments with covered tops, because of fears of top-heaviness, until 1925. Trials were then successful and converted NS buses started to run in service from 1926. Pneumatic tyres were allowed for single-deckers in 1925 and for double-deckers in 1927, and the speed limit for those so fitted was raised from 12 to 20 m.p.h. in 1928.

The central overhaul works at Chiswick was brought into use in 1921–22. Repair and maintenance, previously undertaken at the various garages, could be carried out there more satisfactorily. The time a bus was off the road was reduced from an average of 16 days to 4, thereby increasing the number of vehicles available for service.

Other bus manufacturers, such as Leyland and Guy, looked enviously at

The London bus saw many design improvements during the 1920s: for example, 37 different chassis were built for the LGOC in the 20 years from 1909. Many older vehicles were kept running, however. This K-type, introduced in 1919 and seating 46, was still essentially an adapted horse bus; it was photographed in service passing the National Gallery in 1929. (A modern covered-top vehicle is seen in the background.) The last K-types were withdrawn in 1930. Ref. U5587

the LGOC's AEC-dominated London streets, much as Daimler had done before 1913. Generous hire-purchase terms encouraged independent operators to start up in competition using other makes of bus. Arthur George Partridge, the first of the independents, ran his Chocolate Express from Shepherd's Bush to Liverpool Street from 5 August 1922. By the end of 1923 there were over 150 independent buses operating and the number had risen to 459 by the end of 1924 – almost one in ten of the total licensed.

In 1923 the LGOC reduced its fares from just over to just under a penny a mile, but they were not cut further. Competition was on service, not price. Some of the independents – the 'pirates' – never tried to offer a regular service throughout the day but creamed the traffic at busy times; the worst of them even turned passengers off if they saw a long queue waiting to travel in the opposite direction. But the responsible independents, like Partridge, ran their buses all day to a fixed timetable.

The London Traffic Act (1924) established a licensing authority with powers to limit the number of buses allowed to ply on certain busy streets ('designated' streets) or where an adequate service was provided by alternative forms of transport, mainly tramways. The measure was much influenced by interim recommendations from the departmental Hackney Vehicle Committee, which had been set up in 1922; this had in its turn formed a sub-committee to consider bus routes and services. Frank Pick was the sub-committee's chairman.

The number of independent buses peaked at 556 in November 1925. Then new traffic regulations began to bite as

The NS-type (1923) was designed from the wheels upwards (though the tyres were still solid rubber). The one above was photographed at Wembley on a showery June day in 1924. The addition of covered tops had to wait until the Metropolitan Police gave permission. Refs. H/9570 and U3971

The ST-type which, with the LT, ushered in the 1930s. The driver at last had a windscreen.   Ref. 18309

Larger, six-wheel vehicles dated from 1927. They provided more room on the seats and more leg room. The LT-type (1929) seated 54. Direct competitors with tramcars, they had their uses on straight, wide roads but were not allowed within three miles of Mansion House.   Ref. U5776

Two pirates: (left) Partridge's Leyland Chocolate Express, and (below) one of the Guy buses put on the streets in 1927 by the newly formed London Public Omnibus Company. Refs. 15319 and H/12218

Other independent bus companies ran outside the LGOC's area and had been doing so since before the war. Notable among them was the Reigate-based East Surrey Traction Co. and the National Omnibus and Transport Co. which had developed from Thomas Clarkson's oil-fired steam bus interests, based in Chelmsford. For years LGOC worked in collaboration with these outliers, agreeing routes and boundaries, but when the main-line railways gained bus operating powers in 1928 it decided to take financial control. East Surrey was purchased outright in 1929 and its name was later changed to London General Country Services Ltd. The National Company joined it in January 1932. By then some others had been acquired and many more were to come.

In the meantime coach operators from outside the London area had started to run services into the centre. These were difficult for the LGOC to counter because they were not regulated by the London Traffic Act (1924). It retaliated in 1929 by running its own (or its Home Counties Associates') coaches from places such as Watford, Windsor, Tunbridge Wells and Reigate. Green Line Coaches Ltd was formed in July 1930 to operate these services as a wholly owned LGOC subsidiary. When it became part of London General Country Services in May 1932, the whole undertaking already had a fleet of 808 vehicles and a staff of 6,000.

In these busy and bustling times for passenger transport on the roads, the tramways, which lacked the motor buses' flexibility and access to most of London's central streets, did well just to

the Ministry declared more of London's central streets, and all its roads containing tramways, to be 'designated'. Some of the independents were prepared to sell. By March 1927 the LGOC had acquired 207 of their buses. But in the following July, the London Public Omnibus Company, financed by Clarence Hatry, was registered not only to run its new Guy buses but also to compete with the LGOC in buying out the other independents. Seventy-six companies,

and their 215 buses, were soon acquired. Within a year, however, the LGOC had gained a majority holding in the LPOC. It was wound up at the end of 1929. The smaller survivors, including Birch Brothers, signed 'co-ordinating and withdrawal of competition' agreements and fell into the same category as Thomas Tilling, the Peckham-based business that had done well for itself while working in concert with the LGOC since the 1850s.

A Tilling bus, among others, in Trafalgar Square (South Africa House is on the left and the entrance to the Strand in the centre). The total absence of buses with covered tops or pneumatic tyres indicates that the photograph was taken before 1930.   Ref. H/14732

hold their traffic. Almost the only development in their favour was the rebuilding of the Kingsway tunnel to accommodate double-deck cars; it reopened on 15 January 1931. There was then a true link between the LCC systems north and south of the river.

The tramways' continued popularity arose mainly from their very low fares: the LCC charged about 0.7 pence per mile and the companies just under a penny. The LCC's shilling all-day tramcar tickets were particularly popular among small boys who learned much about London from their top decks. Such low fares were possible only because of an element of subsidy, either

from the local authority or, in the case of the LUT, from the Underground Group.

After many years during which the emphasis had been on modification and rebuilding of the fleet, the Feltham, an improved type of tramcar with better acceleration and braking, went into service with the LUT and MET in 1931. The LUT also began to convert some of its more lightly trafficked south-westerly routes to trolleybus operation. The first of these hybrids began to run between Twickenham Junction and Teddington on 16 May 1931.

It was, however, the buses that generated most of the additional journeys during the 1920s, short though

most of these were. They increased from 932 million in 1921 to 1,958 million in 1930. Local railway (Underground Group and Metropolitan) traffic grew a little, from 588 million journeys a year to 601 million, though these were somewhat longer journeys; the numbers of those on suburban main lines (certainly longer) grew more impressively, from 324 million a year to 423 million. Tramway journeys, more numerous than those by bus in 1921, soon fell far behind, increasing only from 1,009 million a year to 1,087 million. Rides per head of population per year continued to rise in the period, from 382 to 511.

Green Line coaches (below) climbing Westerham Hill in 1931, and (right) at the stop on Eccleston Bridge, behind Victoria station, a few years later.   Refs. U8475 and U24522

(Right) A Feltham tramcar at Ealing Broadway; (middle) an LUT trolleybus at Twickenham in 1931. Refs. U7896 and U8669

Double-deck tramcars on the Victoria Embankment in 1933 (after the enlargement of the Kingsway tunnel), drawing their electrical energy by conduit rather than by overhead wire. There was little other traffic of any kind. Ref. 13650

PROGRESS DURING THE THIRTIES

After 1933 Ashfield, Pick and their staff at the LPTB had more scope than ever to plan the future shape of their business. The railways, vital though they were to the life of London, required such heavy fixed capital investment that they yielded unimpressive returns, and the motor buses made up the Board's main source of income. The 1930s in fact saw the heyday of the Board's buses. Bus competition had been removed and that of motor cars had not yet arrived (fewer than 300,000 cars were licensed in London in 1933), and the conversion of most horse-drawn goods vehicles to faster motor lorries and vans speeded the whole traffic flow.

The continued expansion of London's Underground into the surrounding countryside was made much easier by collaboration with the main-line companies through the new traffic pool. The Joint Standing Committee, formed in 1933, could not have been more impressive: the chief executives of the four main lines together with Ashfield, Pick and two other members of the Board, Patrick Ashley Cooper, who was a director of the Bank of England as well as Governor of the Hudson's Bay Company, and Sir Henry Maybury, the country's leading authority on road engineering. These powerful figures, or their expert deputies, were able to grapple with problems or decide priorities without party political interference.

Underground station reconstruction in the centre was continued on the Piccadilly Line at Knightsbridge, Hyde Park Corner, Green Park, Leicester Square, Holborn and King's Cross, where the booking hall and escalators came into use on 18 July 1939. On the Central Line further work was carried out at Tottenham Court Road, and Chancery Lane and St Paul's were reconstructed. So too was Moorgate.

Some of these major improvements were undertaken as part of a massive New Works Programme, announced in 1935, financed by government-guaranteed loans totalling £40 million and raised in the market at 2½ per cent instead of the prevailing rate of 3¾ per cent, because of the guarantee.

The first of these projects was the removal of the Metropolitan Railway's bottleneck immediately north of its Baker Street station, long considered by that company but more readily soluble now that the Metropolitan was part of the LPTB. It was achieved by building a branch from the Bakerloo north from

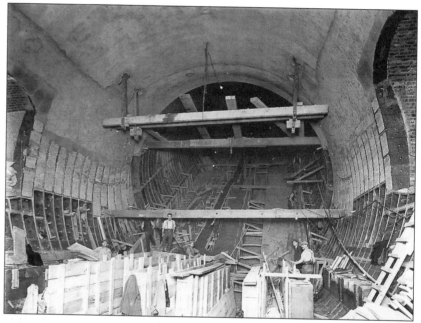

Four escalators in one shaft for the first time on the Underground: the upper flight at Holborn, (above) under construction in November 1932, and (right) two of the escalators in use. Refs. U11669 and U24172

Baker Street, coming to the surface near Finchley Road where there was a cross-platform interchange with the Metropolitan. From there Bakerloo trains ran as slow stoppers along Metropolitan tracks to Wembley Park and then to Stanmore, which had been reached by the Metropolitan in 1932. Metropolitan trains ran express to Wembley Park. This project took some time to realise: a through Bakerloo service to Stanmore did not start until 20 November 1939.

The other major railway schemes involved the LNER and, to a smaller extent, the GWR. The existing LNER lines from Liverpool Street were to be electrified through Stratford, Ilford and Romford to Shenfield, and the LPTB's Central Line was to be extended underground from Liverpool Street to take over the LNER's Loughton, Ongar and Grange Hill/Hainault loop line, with a new tunnel under Eastern Avenue to serve North Ilford. At its western end, the Central was to be extended over new tracks parallel to the GWR's Birmingham line from North Acton through Greenford to West Ruislip. Work began on these schemes, but the lines were not opened to traffic until after the war.

The New Works Programme also included support for LPTB's conversion programme from trams to trolleybuses. It was felt that the massive expense required in updating and renewing the tramway system could not be justified and that trolleybuses could provide many of the advantages at less cost. This included the whole of the Bexley, Dartford, Erith, Ilford, Walthamstow and London United tramways, together with a substantial part of the Croydon, East Ham, Leyton, West Ham, MET and SMET systems and part of the LCC area. During the four years after 1935 the trolleybus route mileage grew from 18

to 236 and that of the tramways fell from 324 to 135. In 1939, however, trams were still responsible for 516 million journeys and trolleybuses 571 million.

The STL bus of 1932 was the LGOC's last design. It appeared in many variations, with seating capacity ranging from 49 to 60; 56 seats were usual. Nearly 2,650 STL buses had been produced by 1937, when the last NS-type was withdrawn. They were originally powered by six-cylinder petrol engines,

ate 'compulsory' and 'request' signs erected. Electric tramways and trolleybus routes had had fixed stops from the beginning.

The bus and coach fleet continued to grow, from 5,976 in 1934 to 6,389 in 1939. The depression of the early 1930s had temporarily halted the upward growth in the number of bus journeys but in 1934 it began rising again, from 1,950 million to 2,230 million in 1939. This was more than twice the number of journeys undertaken by tram and

Rural Stanmore in 1933, a year after it was reached by the Metropolitan Railway. Bakerloo trains started to arrive in 1939, after the completion of the link from Baker Street to Finchley Road.
Ref. 21168

but at the first meeting of the new LPTB the decision was taken to change to the more economical oil engines, popularly known as diesels.

Although London buses had fixed stages, it was customary to hail them at will to stop between these points, as one does taxis today. The 'fixed stop' system was started on 20 March 1935, and then only experimentally, on the road between Euston Road and Seven Sisters, Tottenham. It was extended before the war to 380 route miles, but a further 970 miles still had to have the appropri-

trolleybus in the latter year (516 million and 571 million respectively). Underground traffic grew from 416 million to 473 million journeys and main-line suburban traffic from 526 million to 587 million journeys over the same period.

The motor bus clearly led the way. Ashfield once remarked that his business depended on pairs of men, one at the front and one at the back of a series of moving platforms. It certainly cannot be over-emphasised that it was the motor bus that made the LPTB viable.

Part of the vast New Works Programme announced in 1935: the tunnel entrance to the Northern Line being built at East Finchley in February 1938 to link Archway with the LNER line to High Barnet. The line was extended to East Finchley on 3 July 1939 and to High Barnet on 14 April 1940, and the branch from Finchley Central to Mill Hill East on 18 May 1940. The further extension from Mill Hill East to Edgware and Bushey Heath, upon which much work had been done, was postponed and never taken up again.   Ref. 16826

Part of the large conversion from tramcars to trolleybuses: Tally Ho, North Finchley, in 1939.   Ref. U30541

An STL bus in May 1935, here seen in light traffic at Marble Arch. The driver now had a cab over which the top deck was extended to provide a few more seats for passengers.
Ref. U17307

An early bus request stop, 1936. Until then, although there were fare stages, passengers could hail a bus anywhere along the route.
Ref. U24361

THE SECOND WORLD WAR

Londons buses were not commandeered for service at the Front in the Second World War as they had been in the First, but 400 Green Line coaches were converted for use as ambulances and several disused Underground stations in central London were made available for use by the government, the Railway Executive and London Transport itself. It helped to move 607,000 evacuees in four days on the outbreak of war and a further group of over 110,000 in the six days after 13 June 1940, when the Battle of Britain was about to begin. More were moved later, especially during the V1 (flying bomb) and V2 (rocket) attacks in 1944–45: in all over 1,250,000 evacuees throughout the war.

London Transport's property – its garages and stations – and its road and rail network, spread out over the whole of the metropolis, were more exposed to the full force of German bombing than the premises and plant of any other single business. But its underground railways and stations not only provided much protection but also offered shelter from the bombing to thousands of Londoners. Although at the outbreak of war electrically operated floodgates were installed in the tubes to protect them from being inundated, it was impossible to prevent human tragedy when the Underground suffered a direct hit elsewhere. London Transport witnessed some of the capital's worst disasters.

Between August 1940 and July 1941 nearly 40,000 high explosive bombs and millions of incendiaries fell on London. These were followed, between June 1944 and March 1945, by 2,430 V1 flying bombs and 570 V2 rockets (249 V1s and 75 V2s fell either

Evacuation of London schoolchildren by train, in September 1939.   Ref. 19447

on London Transport premises or near enough to damage them). In all, 166 buses and coaches, 69 trams, 15 trolleybuses and 19 railway carriages were destroyed and thousands more damaged. Sixty-five of the buses were destroyed at Croydon garage on the night of Saturday 10 May 1941, the worst night of the blitz so far as London Transport was concerned. There were 20 direct hits on its railways, its tunnels were pierced at four places and its tracks blocked at nine points. The next day no

bus route could be operated through central London nor any tram route to the inner termini south of the river (and only to one terminus north of it). Yet on the Monday morning buses covered all the interrupted tram routes and all services were 'substantially restored' within ten days, apart from a stretch of the Circle between King's Cross and Euston which was out of action for five months.

Tube stations served as shelters after the first major night raid on 7

Early bomb damage at Clapham tram sheds,
1941.   Ref. U32892

The passengers and crew of this bus had
fortunately gone to a nearby public shelter on
the sounding of the air raid warning one
night in September 1940. The bomb blast
hurled the bus into the air and it fell against
the first floor windows of a terrace of houses.
Ref. H/17281

In the very heart of London, the scene at the Bank station after a bomb had penetrated the underground concourse. Ref. 23055

Severe air raid damage (below) at Croydon Garage, 1941. Ref. U33042

During the early phases of the night blitz, people sought shelter on station platforms and even on the escalators . . .
Refs. 24601 and 24782

. . . but later (bottom photograph was taken in November 1943) bunks were provided – 22,800 altogether at the various tube stations. There were not enough for everyone, however. Ref. 24782

September 1940. Shelters were eventually provided at 79 tube stations, with accommodation for 75,000 people. But shelter was not always synonymous with safety. One terrible incident occurred at Balham on 14 October 1940. A bomb penetrated the northbound station tunnel and a water main burst, killing 60 people sheltering in the station. At the Bank in January 1941 a bomb penetrated the roadway and burst in the concourse underground, destroying the booking office and wrecking the escalators. The blast damaged two trains in the station 62 feet below, and 53 shelterers and four staff died. In all during the war 181 London Transport staff were killed on duty and 1,867 were more or less seriously injured.

London Transport formed part of the London Aircraft Production Group, which, amongst other things, produced more than 700 Halifax bombers in LT's workshops. It also built bridging pontoons, assembled and tested lorries and overhauled armoured vehicles. Five miles of the new, but still unused, Central Line extension between Leytonstone and Gants Hill were turned into an aircraft components factory, completed in March 1942.

Of the regular staff, 22,500 left for full-time service in the armed forces or civil defence; by the end of the war 16,500 women were carrying out jobs formerly done by men.

Evacuation, the blackout and air attacks reduced the number of passenger journeys in 1940 and 1941 by nearly 25 per cent; but they then started to

Tragedy struck at Balham in 1940. A direct hit in the street above destroyed a water main and killed 60 people sheltering in the station below. Refs. 22226 and U31956

pick up again as more people returned to London or passed through it. In 1945 the number of journeys was only 3 per cent below the 1938–39 figure.

Frank Pick died on 7 November 1941, just before his sixty-third birthday. He had left the LPTB the previous year and had served briefly as Director General of the Ministry of Information. Sir John Elliot wrote in a well-informed assessment in the *Dictionary of National Biography*:

> *It was the combination of Pick and Ashfield, rather than the work of either, that brought about the remarkable development of public passenger transport in London in the 30 years prior to the outbreak of war in 1939. The two men were essentially complementary. Ashfield was at his best in dealing with politicians, shareholders and the public. Pick, on the other hand, was a very shy man, but he had great qualities as an administrator. He was primarily responsible for the day-to-day efficiency of the system which technically was generally acknowledged to be without equal anywhere in the world.*

Ashfield reached the age of 70 in 1944, and remained LPTB chairman until October 1947, that is to say, almost to its dying day at the end of that year. On 1 January 1948 he did not become a member of the London Transport Executive but of its overlord, the British Transport Commission. He died within the year, on 4 November 1948.

(Top) Plessey's wartime factory at Redbridge. Ref. U33281

Women (middle) as bus conductors again, from November 1940, and (left) working in the engineering shops. Refs. 22845 and 24780

Part Four

London Transport Loses Its Lead

Prince Charles opens the Jubilee Line to Charing Cross in 1979.
Ref. 18720

A FADING OPTIMISM

At the end of the war the LPTB still headed the largest and busiest unified transport system in the world. It employed almost 100,000 people and, together with the main-line railways' suburban services, was responsible for passenger travel over an area within a 25-mile radius of Charing Cross with a residential population of nearly ten million, as well as a vast inflow of visitors to the capital for business or pleasure. Physical wartime damage was soon made good. Nevertheless, some provincial buses had to be hired for a time until new vehicles became available; the shortage was overcome by 1950.

LPTB inherited a clear policy, which had been laid down in 1933. The Underground was to be extended farther into the suburbs and beyond, and more spacious stations were to be built in the centre to handle the increasing concentration of traffic there. Petrol buses were to be replaced by oil (diesel) and new bus services were to be introduced, especially in suburban districts and the newly built-up areas beyond. The trams were to be replaced by trolleybuses.

Much of the rest of the New Works Programme of 1935 – the extensions of the Central Line tube eastwards to join the London & North Eastern's tracks and westwards in collaboration with the

(Above) Poster advertising the extension of the Central Line to Leytonstone in May 1947, and (right) the new station there. From December 1947 onwards Central Line trains ran along two branches, one to Newbury Park using tubes built much earlier (part of which had been used by Plessey between 1942 and 1945 as an aircraft component factory – see page 104) and the other to Woodford by electrified LNER surface line, which had already brought the railway from the tube exit at Leyton to Leytonstone. Hainault was reached from both Newbury Park and Woodford during 1948. Refs. U48135 and U47326

Great Western – was completed in 1949. The last electric trams were withdrawn in 1952. Proposals were made for more tubes, notably Route C, eventually to be better known as the Victoria Line. Morale at London Transport was high and traffic by both road and rail reached a peak in 1948. There were as yet no worries about labour shortages. The tone of the annual reports was distinctly optimistic.

But not for long; and their growing

CENTRAL LINE
EASTERN **EXTENSION**
◯→ **OPEN MAY 5** ⟨LNER⟩
THROUGH TRAINS FROM THE WEST END AND CITY

pessimism was well founded, as is very evident when we, with the benefit of hindsight, compare the very modest achievements of the last forty years with the remarkable developments of the previous forty. Why was the steady investment in the Underground not maintained? And why did the traffic on London Transport's road services fall by the end of the 1980s to little more than a quarter of its postwar total?

It is true that the postwar management has not so far produced a team comparable to that of Stanley and Pick: no postwar chairman or general manager has served so long in office, nor been able to exercise the public influence that Stanley was able to do after his experience in government during the First World War. Here is part of the answer to our question. Stanley brought his influence to bear on the politicians, rather than vice versa. He secured their help in obtaining low-interest loans, but did not in return surrender any freedom to manage his business. The Board was appointed by independent trustees. This was no longer the case after 1948.

The LPTB hoped to escape nationalisation, but the Labour government thought otherwise. The Board suffered a

double blow by being at once national-ised and demoted to the status of an Executive of that unwieldy, ill-selected and in due course extinct leviathan, the British Transport Commission. Ashfield, one of the ill-selected (he was 73 years old at the time), was in no position to help his old firm, and in any case he died within a few months of his appointment. The BTC did not influence the London Transport Executive's day-to-day run-ning; but it could, and did, delay major investment decisions. These had to fit in with a broader national railway prog-ramme, and the main lines saw to it that they were given higher priority. Moreover, members of the Executive were no longer appointed by indepen-dent trustees but by the Minister. There was, however, strong continuity for some time between the LPTB and the new Executive. The traditions and style of Ashfield and Pick persisted. Neverthe-less, both Conservative and Labour governments delayed some very neces-sary fare increases on national economic grounds.

THE BUSES SUFFER FROM FULL EMPLOYMENT AND ROAD CONGESTION

Operating conditions started to become harder for London Transport in the 1950s. In London more than elsewhere public transport became a victim of greater national prosperity and full employ-ment.

On the one hand, recruitment became more difficult when plenty of assured jobs became available elsewhere that did not involve shift work in the early hours or late at night. By 1954 efforts were being made to recruit bus drivers and conductors in the provinces

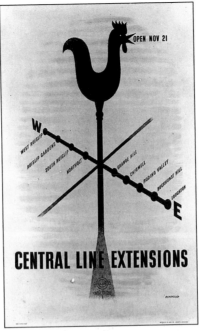

The extension of the Central Line to the north-east reached Loughton in 1948, and was balanced to the north-west by the new service from Greenford to West Ruislip, opened on the same day. The North Acton–Greenford extension had been opened for traffic on 30 June 1947. Both these sections of railway were built by the GWR.
Ref. U45524

and Northern Ireland – and, before long, in Barbados.

On the other hand, greater afflu-ence affected travel habits. The intro-duction of the five-day week deprived London Transport of its Saturday com-muters. More serious was the effect of television on off-peak traffic. (There were very few viewers when the BBC television service was resumed from Alexandra Palace after the war, but when the first ITV channel was started in 1955 an estimated 40 per cent of London households had sets.) People went out less at night and at weekends. Off-peak buses and trains grew emptier.

Even more serious for London Transport, many more people began to run their own motor cars. Car owner-ship had hardly concerned the old LPTB. Only 426,000 cars were licensed in London and the five home counties in

1935, and only a few more than that in 1950 when petrol rationing ended. But thereafter the number of vehicles licensed in the London area began to grow quickly: from 480,000 (1950) to 803,000 (1955), over 1,275,000 (1960) and more than 2,100,000 (1967). By 1954 London Transport was obliged to assemble a team of inspectors to turn buses on certain routes. Later street scenes tell their own story of congestion and delay.

Congestion in the centre often slowed buses there to speeds little better than those in horse-bus days. Traffic engineering (one-way streets, timed traffic lights and other expedients) was introduced in 1960 in an attempt to speed the flow of vehicles, but there were accompanying disadvantages: within a one-way system many would-be passengers had to walk some distance to find a bus route, let alone a bus stop. When the stop was reached, a long wait might ensue (bad enough in warm, fine weather but much worse when it was cold and wet). Then several buses often arrived simultaneously: the London bus, in the memorable words of Flanders and Swann, had become 'most gregarious'. It acquired a bad name with the travel-ling public, and traffic went on falling. The service was then cut to save costs – and, as it deteriorated, lost more traffic. This was what London Transport came to call its 'vicious spiral'. Between 1948 and 1962 the number of passengers carried by its road services fell from 3,955 million to 2,485 million. But, ever since the merger of 1912, it had always been the buses that had pro-duced most of its profit. This deteriora-tion therefore struck a mortal blow at the financial viability of the whole undertaking.

Until the mid-1960s, however, London Transport's railways and buses

In this picture of Epping station (below), a steam shuttle service is seen operating to Ongar – this section of line was not electrified until November 1957. Sitting alongside is an electric train operating to Ealing Broadway.   Refs. U47869 and U54663

Last Tram Week (1952), after which cars were withdrawn from the remaining routes. This tram is picking up passengers in Lewisham. Ref. 19659/4

A trolleybus in traffic at Harlesden. Trolleybuses did not survive for much longer than trams; the last one finally returned to depot on 8 May 1962. Ref. 13936

The new London Transport Executive that succeeded the LPTB on 1 January 1948. Lord Latham (seated centre) had been an LPTB member since 1937 and left the leadership of the LCC to become the Executive's chairman. The other full-time members had all been LPTB principal officers: (seated left to right) L. C. Hawkins, John Cliff (deputy chairman), A. H. Grainger and A. B. B. Valentine. Of the part-time members (standing left to right), T. E. Williams, Sir Richard Burbidge and Sir Edward Hardy, the last-named had also been an LPTB member. Ref. 24781

managed to maintain an adequate working surplus, the road services contributing about £3–4 million a year to this and the Underground a little over £1 million. But towards the end of his chairmanship (1959–65) Sir Alec Valentine, who had worked for the undertaking since 1928 and had been on its first Executive, was sounding serious notes of alarm. The bus services were about to start losing money.

Traffic engineering had merely encouraged more vehicles to fill the extra road space it released. Congestion had

in by road at busy times – as they had done successfully between the 1920s and the later 1940s. But polite exhortation was as far as it was prepared to go. An Ashfield, one thinks, would have had more to say both in private and, through his public relations department, in public. Ironically, just as the most recent versions of the London bus had become technically more efficient, more spacious and more comfortable than ever, it was no longer permitted to perform the function for which it had been developed.

Transport Executive, now called the London Transport Board, could deal directly with the Ministry of Transport. Sir Alec Valentine, who had himself been a member of the BTC, subsequently complained that its intermediacy had delayed unnecessarily the sanction of large-scale investment in the Underground. Two particular cases were cited: the modernisation of Lots Road power station, LT's main supplier of electricity – first put forward in 1952, approved only in 1962 and completed in 1968 – and the Victoria Line. The latter provided much-needed railway capacity from north-east London, linked the main-line termini at King's Cross, St Pancras, Euston and Victoria, and greatly improved underground travel in the centre too. The story of its delayed authorisation is a cautionary tale.

The idea had originated as Route C in a group of recommendations put forward by the LPTB immediately after the war. The BTC selected it in 1948 as the preferred route in the group and gave the London Transport Executive authority to publish and even to publicise it, but did not hold out any prospect

Trafalgar Square in 1952: buses still dominate the traffic scene. By this time, the vast majority of LT's bus services were being handled by the RT bus type. First introduced before the war and afterwards mass-produced until more than 7,000 were in use by 1954; the RT and its variants served London for 40 years. Ref. 17600

become as severe as ever at certain times of day, and those times grew longer. The introduction of parking meters from 1958 may have discouraged some drivers from bringing their cars into London, but it did not persuade people to return to the buses.

In its annual reports London Transport stressed that buses alone could cope with the volume of traffic coming

A PROMISING INTERVAL

Despite the prospect of the lucrative bus revenues turning to loss, the 1960s were not without their brighter side; and for a brief moment in the early 1970s it seemed that a serious attempt might be made to come to grips with road congestion.

The British Transport Commission was abolished in 1962 and the London

A recruiting poster of 1954. Ref. H/5443

of finance. In 1959, however, £1,000,000 was found to build twin tunnels along the section of the route between Finsbury Park and Seven Sisters, in order to experiment with new types of tunnel lining. This stretch was built in 1961–62. Fortunately for London, the government was becoming concerned about the threat of unemployment in north-east England and

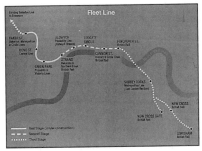

London Transport's proposal for the Fleet Line, published in its Annual Report *for 1971.* Ref. 24778

anxious to create work there. In answer to enquiries received during the summer of 1962, London Transport was able to give assurances that some of the work on the tunnel segments would be subcontracted in the north-east. For this rather distant reason, the whole of the Victoria Line was at last authorised.

It was opened from Walthamstow Central to Highbury and Islington on 1 September 1968, to Warren Street on 1 December and to Victoria on 7 March 1969. The extension south of the river to Brixton, decided upon in 1965, followed on 23 July 1971 and the final station at Pimlico was completed in September 1972.

(Above right) A Victoria Line train entering Seven Sisters station. Fully automated, the line was technically the most advanced in the world. One operator, acting as both driver and guard, could open and close the doors and start the train by activating the automatic control mechanism. (Right) The railway also had automatic ticket issue, and entry to stations was by special gates operated by tickets with a magnetically encoded backing. Refs. 14384–5 and H/16441

The significance of this important addition to London's Underground was emphasised by the official opening (of the Victoria section) by the Queen, the first time that a reigning monarch had opened any part of the system.

The 14-mile Victoria Line, built at a total cost of £91 million, contained railway interchanges at almost all of its 16 stations. It spread the traffic and speeded up journeys, especially that between King's Cross and Victoria, which was cut from about 24 minutes to ten. Within two months of its opening to Victoria the line was carrying passengers at the rate of 58 million a year; 12 months later this total had risen to 82 million – nor was this at the expense of other lines on the system, for passenger mileage as a whole increased. The most

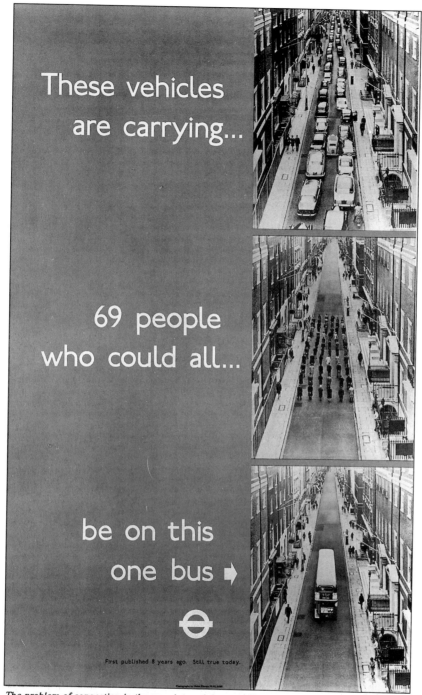

The problem of congestion in the morning rush hour, as London Transport saw it in 1965.
Ref. H/16491

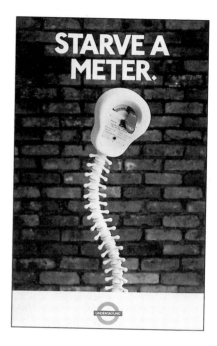

closer relationship being established between BR and LT. No less significant, work had started a few months before on the 3½-mile extension of the Piccadilly Line from Hounslow West to Heathrow Airport.

So far as the Underground was concerned, it seemed as if London Transport was about to catch up on many years of little more than piecemeal improvement and care and maintenance. Operating surpluses, £1 million a year in the mid-1960s, rose to £4 million in 1970 and £21 million in 1973. The buses, on the other hand, were starting to return losses of £5 million and more in the mid-1960s. By 1973 these losses had risen to £11 million.

In 1966 the Board decided to try to reduce these bus losses by moving to one-man operation and shortened routes. An experimental flat-fare single-deck Red Arrow service was introduced in April 1966 between Victoria and Marble Arch, and in July 1968 an agreement was reached with the Transport and General Workers Union to

obvious weakness of this otherwise well planned and executed undertaking was the underground concourse at Victoria, which was designed far too small for the volume of traffic it had to handle.

London Transport had high hopes that the new underground line would be followed by others. The first stage of what was to be called the Fleet Line, from Baker Street to Charing Cross, was authorised in August 1971. So were British Railways' plans for the electrification of their Great Northern suburban services from Moorgate, using the old main-line-sized Great Northern & City tube of 1904, a good example of the

operate these single-deckers more extensively. By the end of 1969 517 of them were at work and experiments had also been carried out with front-entrance double-deckers, manned only by the driver. By the end of 1970, 35 one-man double-deckers and nearly 800 single-deckers were in daily service on 95 routes. Between 1964 and 1970 the numbers employed in the operating and servicing of London's buses fell from 45,000 to 32,000, which accounted for almost the whole of the fall from 74,000 to 60,000 in London Transport's total staff during those years. It soon came to be realised, however, that single manning could not be extended to double-deckers on central routes at peak hours because of the long delays at stops while fares were collected.

Another change in political control was on the way. On 1 April 1965 the Greater London Council replaced the London County Council. It had responsibility for major non-trunk roads in London (trunk roads were the Ministry's responsibility) and for traffic management throughout an area more extensive than that of its predecessor. In 1967 the energetic Labour Minister of Transport, Barbara Castle, reached a remarkable private agreement with Desmond Plummer, Leader of the Conservative-controlled GLC, whereby responsibility for London Transport would pass from central government (which had acquired it on the abolition of the BTC in 1962) to the Council. By an Act passed two years later the GLC became LT's political and financial master from the beginning of 1970. The Board became an Executive once more.

Single manning had been intended to cut operating costs. Separate bus lanes, introduced soon afterwards, were an attempt to speed services. They were introduced very tentatively. The first

two, one down Park Lane and the other across Vauxhall Bridge, were tried out in 1968, but at first only during evening peak hours. A third, in Brixton Road during the morning rush, did not follow until 1970. One more was introduced in 1971, northbound along the Albert Embankment. 'Progress,' London Transport ruefully reported in 1971, 'is still slow' and, in the following year, even more despondently: 'Although further traffic engineering schemes, clearways [including the six-months' experimental closure of Oxford Street west of Oxford Circus between 11.00 a.m. and 11.00 p.m. from October], parking controls and bus lanes were introduced during

1972, these useful but generally isolated measures were not being introduced boldly or quickly enough to combat the strangling effects of private cars and lorries.'

The best-known bus lane, the contraflow down Piccadilly, had been under consideration for years and eventually came into use in April 1973. By the end of that year there were 45 bus lanes in operation altogether at rush hour, though LT complained about their lax supervision. There was not much success in keeping even the bus stops clear of parked traffic. The Speedbus Network put forward in the 1973 *Annual Report* seemed a very futuristic notion indeed.

One of London's first bus lanes was designated along Park Lane in 1968. Ref. 19335

London Transport's Annual Report *for 1972 contrasted (right) Oxford Street looking west from Oxford Circus with cars excluded with (below) the view looking east with buses held up by cars and commercial traffic – both of which were soon, at least nominally, excluded in both directions.*   Ref. 46638

The contraflow bus lane down Piccadilly (1973) was protected by a pavement as well as a white line. The Routemaster bus – which dominates this view – was not only the last to be designed 'in-house' by LT to suit its needs, but also the last type of traditional open rear platform bus to remain in service in Britain. The advanced design, incorporating many aluminium chassis components in order to save weight, represented the peak of conventional bus design. The fast loading and unloading potential of the open platform design and their popularity with the public has slowed down the replacement of the Routemaster by more modern types. Several hundred remained in service on some of the most congested routes in 1990, more than 35 years after their introduction. Ref. 24771

The beginning of flat-fare single manning: a Red Arrow single-decker at Victoria station in 1966. Single-manned double-deckers were introduced five years later.   Ref. 21474

For a brief spell in the early 1970s, however, with the GLC in charge of both roads and LT, and with the sympathetic Heath Conservative government operating in an encouraging economic climate, there was an opportunity for the previous policy of decline and retrenchment to be reversed.

London's buses featured quite prominently in 1972 during a Commons enquiry into urban transport planning, carried out by a sub-committee of the

cate a greater proportion of the existing road space to the bus by establishing bus lanes.'

At last there was a current of support from Parliament, allying itself with the GLC to back a policy that London Transport had long been advocating. In its *Annual Report* for 1972 the Executive repeated in a different form the message of the 1965 poster. Many more cars were entering London in the morning rush but fewer people

its own, is shown in a revealing passage from a discussion of its sources of income in its report for the previous year:

> *The extent to which these payments [for its transport services] should come from fares, from rates, from a transport tax on the Paris model, or from other sources of finance, is at the heart of the public debate. This is a matter of politics and financial policy on which it would be improper for the Executive to adopt any stance or to express any views. Its duty is to do its utmost to run the best public transport system that can be achieved within the policy set down for it in the Transport (London) Act 1969 and by the Greater London Council.*

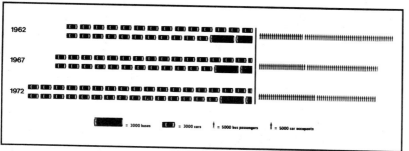

1962

1967

1972

= 3000 buses   = 3000 cars   = 5000 bus passengers   = 5000 car occupants

Between 1962 and 1972 the number of cars using the roads into Central London during the morning peak increased substantially but there was a fall in the number of people carried.

Expenditure Committee. Much evidence was given in support of the view that it was reliability rather than price that dictated the extent to which public transport was used. The sub-committee concentrated upon road congestion, the main cause of delay. There was support, especially from Christopher Foster, the cost/benefit specialist who had helped to advise on the economic feasibility of the Victoria Line and had been Barbara Castle's Director General of Economic Planning, in favour of giving priority to buses and restricting car traffic.

Congestion was by no means due entirely to the private car: 95 per cent of London's goods deliveries arrived by road. Nevertheless the sub-committee reached the clear conclusion that '*national policy should be directed towards promoting public transport and discouraging the use of cars for the journey to work in city areas*. Local authorities should be required to allo-

were coming in by road. 'There can be little doubt,' the report observed, 'of the growing recognition in all quarters of the essential future role that public transport has to play' and it cited the Expenditure Committee's second report as marking 'a major step forward in the process. Many of the recommendations in that Report give general endorsement, for the first time, to views which in the past have been regarded as biased and axe-grinding pronouncements from professional public transport practitioners'. The Expenditure Committee's recommendations were reproduced in full as an appendix to the report.

Unfortunately London Transport, even with such influential all-party backing, did not seize this remarkable opportunity to use its public relations department to plead its case more loudly and publicly. That it now regarded itself solely as responsible for carrying out the policies of others rather than pursuing

Times had indeed changed since the days of Ashfield and Pick.

So the Executive stood aside and watched its own lucrative bus traffic go on declining. There were one or two initiatives worthy of note. Bonuses to bus crews, related to fares collected, resulted in improved timekeeping (1970). Cheap, off-peak travel for pensioners and the disabled, introduced for Camden residents in 1970, was extended to other boroughs by the end of 1971, the necessary LT permits being paid for by the boroughs concerned. This off-peak travel became free on the buses from 1973; by the end of the year, 875,000 elderly Londoners had free passes. Regular sightseeing tours for the increasing number of visitors to London quickly became popular. Four 16-seat minibuses, introduced experimentally in 1972, were the precursors of the 26-seat 'midibuses' tried out in 1974 and the dial-a-bus service from Golders Green station. The use of smaller vehicles for

An open-top sightseeing bus in 1972. LT utilised elderly, secondhand vehicles for this purpose. Ref. 21459

The dial-a-bus service, started experimentally in 1974 from Golders Green station to the previously bus-free Hampstead Garden Suburb, used radio-equipped minibuses at 15p a journey. Ref. 48503

THE GOING GETS HARDER

In 1973 the Conservatives lost control at County Hall and handed over to a moderate Labour Council, led by Sir Reginald Goodwin. But relations between LT and the GLC were already beginning to deteriorate. The atmosphere of economic optimism and Conservative support for public transport evaporated after the Heath government's fall in 1974.

It might be imagined that Labour in power both at County Hall and over the river at Westminster augured well for LT. It certainly seemed so at first; for the new Council quickly abandoned inner ring road schemes and spoke out strongly in favour of public transport, better road management and more effective vehicle restraint. Very soon, however, the climate began to change as the GLC had at last to face economic reality. Grants to cover LT's losses were growing year by year, and by 1975 both it and the government decided that passengers, not tax- or ratepayers, should foot more of the bill. There were 56 per cent fare increases that year and a further 25 per cent in the next. Although traffic had held up well on both the buses and the Underground during the subsidy period, it now fell back. The *closure* of several bus lanes was another sign of the times. The gloom was further heightened by the Moorgate tube disaster on 28 February 1975, when a train hit the buffers at speed and 43 people died.

The two extensions to the tube system came into service in the later 1970s. The Piccadilly Line extension from Hounslow West to Heathrow was opened on 16 December 1977. Progress on the proposed Fleet Line was delayed, however. The heady hopes of the early 1970s of extending it into the City and

specialist services and to provide access to streets inaccessible to conventional vehicles has since this time become a major facet of LT's operations. Prepayment of fares was greatly extended: discounted strips of tickets were issued for use on flat-fare services and, in June 1972, monthly and annual Red Bus season tickets were first made available, together with four-day, seven-day, monthly and annual 'Go as you please tickets' available on bus and tube.

On the operating side, direct radio links with bus drivers were first introduced on one route in 1970 and soon extended to others. This complemented the tall roadside BESIs (Bus Electronic Scanning Indicators), which had already appeared at intervals along the pavements of the main routes to monitor the position of each bus. CARLA (Computer Assisted Radio Location Aid), introduced in 1973, identified the whereabouts of every bus on a given route by automated analysis of coded signals from each vehicle.

beyond came to nothing. Stage One of what was now known as the Jubilee Line, from Baker Street to Charing Cross, was at last opened on 30 April 1979, not even in jubilee year. From Baker Street trains ran along the Stanmore branch of the former Bakerloo Line.

The promise of the early 1970s had faded by the end of the decade. Despite all efforts at economy, public grants to cover the depreciation and renewal of LT's assets went on rising as inflation gathered pace. Grants for fare relief had been cut back, however, and this re-

On the Buses it's free.

On the Tube 20p.

An Elderly Person's GLC Travel Permit
Off-peak it gives you free bus travel and a maximum single fare of 20p anywhere on the Tube.

Concessionary off-peak travel for the elderly began in the early 1970s. Ref. 24795

started the decline in bus traffic, temporarily halted in the earlier part of the decade. The annual number of bus journeys had fallen from 2,485 million in 1962 and just under 2,000 million in 1966 to 1,500 million or a little fewer in the early 1970s; by 1979 it had dropped below 1,250 million, and was still falling. By the early 1980s it was little more than 1,000 million.

Matters were made worse by the misfortunes of the Underground. As we

saw, it had been making an increasingly valuable contribution to LT's finances in the early 1970s with greater passenger mileage (reaching nearly 3,250 million in 1973, although the number of journeys had by then fallen to 644 million). Now it was losing both money and traffic because of the fare increases. The number of journeys was down to 599 million in 1979 and the passenger mileage to 2,774 million – and falling steeply (to 498 million journeys and 2,275 million passenger miles in 1982).

THE TROUBLED AND EVENTFUL 1980s

During the 1980s London Transport came under the spotlight of publicity to an unprecedented degree. The travelling public had previously taken its services for granted, grumbling when trains did not arrive or when bus journeys were unusually long or unpleasant but rarely taking any other action. Any irate traveller who wrote a letter to a newspaper received a prompt and polite reply from LT's Chief Public Relations Officer, usually containing plausible explanations and closing the matter.

But London Transport's growing difficulties inevitably brought it into the public eye during a troubled and turbulent decade when one chairman was dismissed and another resigned, when new fare arrangements were introduced which vastly increased Underground traffic, with consequent overcrowding, and when above all the tragic fire disaster at King's Cross drew everyone's attention to the extent of LT's underfunding. The subsequent very long inquiry revealed remarkable shortcomings in the management of stations and, many of the public must have thought, in the undertaking as a whole.

In their historical context,

however, these much publicised events do not loom so important. They are rather the predictable outcome of earlier policies which were not widely reported at the time. It is not proposed to consider them in detail here, therefore, nor to mention the personalities concerned. That will be the work of a future historian. Our task will be to reveal the main developments of the 1980s that resulted from London Transport's deteriorating economic circumstances as seen within our longer time perspective.

The two parties at County Hall pursued, as one would expect, different policies to deal with LT's mounting crisis with operating costs growing and traffic revenues falling. The Conservatives, who gained control of the GLC in 1977, soon found themselves putting up fares at a rate exceeding that of the rise in the cost of living. At the same time they were advocating administrative reorganisation – outside consultants were called in – and an economy drive in what they saw as a large, sprawling and inefficient business. Eventually they adopted a policy of breaking down the vast organisation into smaller parts so that each part could be more closely controlled. This kind of reconstruction was fashionable in business at that time.

A Bus Board was brought into being in 1979, with a managing director and eight geographical divisions, each with its own general manager. It was followed in 1980 by a Rail Board, with four divisions (Central and Bakerloo Lines; District and Piccadilly; Metropolitan and Jubilee; Northern and Victoria) and a Property Board, both similarly staffed. There were also separate committees for catering, commercial advertising, London Transport's international consulting activities, and the newly opened London Transport Museum.

A much more radical Labour majority, returned to County Hall in May 1981, within six months had introduced sensational fare reductions, on average 30 per cent (at a time when inflation was running at 20 per cent). These were widely publicised with the slogan 'Fares Fair'. They brought about only a 9 per cent growth in traffic – quite insufficient to make good the revenue lost by the fare reductions. More had to be provided by subsidy. This had been brought down to under 30 per cent by the Conservatives: it now shot up to 54 per cent, more than Paris and Chicago were contributing in support of their transport undertakings though less than Copenhagen, Stockholm, Brussels or New York. One of the local authorities expected to foot the bill was Bromley, a south London borough unserved by the Underground. Its council challenged the legality of the GLC's decision. It lost its case, but appealed successfully to the House of Lords in December 1981. Fares had to be raised again in March 1982, by no less than 96 per cent. Passengers were lost again.

The unfortunate effects of such violent swings in policy helped the House of Commons Transport Committee to recommend the creation of a new metropolitan transport authority, quite independent of the GLC. A sympathetic Thatcher government, returned to power with an increased majority in 1983, was not slow to adopt this recommendation. London Regional Transport came into legal existence on 1 April 1984 as a holding company with the bus and rail boards transformed into limited companies, operating their networks quite independently of each other though collaborating closely on fares and interchange points. To enable the costs of bus maintenance to be more closely controlled, Bus Engineering Ltd was set up to take over this work at

arm's length from operations. The new organisation began trading on 1 April 1985. The one full-time and six part-time members appointed to the old Executive by the GLC in July 1983, who caused much difficulty in its dying months, were replaced on the new LRT Board by seven new part-time members and a deputy chairman, who each added specialist expertise to that of the chairman, finance member and managing directors (bus and railway). Politicians gave way to the better informed.

LRT was fortunate in inheriting a basic change in the method of fare

The 'midibus' tried out in 1974 between Archway and Cricklewood.   Ref. 49898

charging which had been developed quietly and undramatically during all the upsets and change. Experiments with flat 25p fares on one-man buses in the boroughs of Harrow and Havering in 1980 succeeded in attracting more passengers without financial loss. This surprised LT. Zonal charging was extended on 5 April 1981 to the buses in all areas to within three miles of central London. In the following October, when the Fares Fair policy came in, central London was divided into three bus zones

(Inner London, West End and City) and the Underground into two (West End and City), with Underground journeys outside these zones continuing to be charged on a graduated scale according to distance. In May 1983 zoning was extended to the whole of the Underground. The old West End and City zones were then combined for both buses and Underground to form a new Central Zone, with three concentric rings, roughly three miles apart, making four additional rail fare zones covering roughly the whole of the outer bus zone. The effect of this was to reduce Underground fares by an average of 25 per cent, the largest advantage going to those who travelled the longest distance. London Transport, which in earlier days had wherever possible charged the same fares by bus and tube over the same route, was now using all its ingenuity to charge what the market would bear – and to attract more customers. It was charging equally for bus and train in the centre where distances were relatively short and the bus, despite congestion, still had some

The bus control centre at Mansion House in 1972, showing the new bus location equipment for Route 11.   Ref. 1299C

A DMS – a single-man operation, automatic door bus – in operation in Cannon Street, January 1971.   Ref. 15109

A poster issued in 1980, stressing the advantages of the tube service to Heathrow . . .   Ref. 24796

. . . and another issued two years later. London Transport had started two Airbus services in November 1980. These replaced those previously operated by British Airways.

advantages, and unequally farther out, where the four-zone train had the advantage for those in a hurry. The single big Outer Zone, however, attracted those to the cheaper bus who were not so pressed for time, although the minimum fare had been increased. And the zoning system, of course, gave scope for variation: for instance, fares could be lower or higher at certain times of day.

The greatest advantage of the new arrangements, however, was the replacement of most Underground season tickets and bus passes with a range of travelcards, valid on both bus and Underground, allowing passengers freedom of interchange without financial penalty. At the same time, BR season ticket holders were able to book a through ticket to LT's central zone at a 25 per cent discounted fare on LT, an advantage extended in January 1985 by one-day Capitalcards available on both BR and LT. Travelcards did not have to be bought from booking offices but could be picked up at shops. They were an immediate success: 600,000 travelcards and bus passes had been sold by the end of 1983. LRT benefited from the extension of prepayment not only in the additional revenue from traffic gained but also because it was a guarantee against fraud, the extent of which was of growing concern. In the early 1980s, LT itself estimated that it was losing £15 million a year on the buses and £10 million more on the Underground from the activities of fare dodgers and dishonest staff members. In 1983 alone 6,700 Underground passengers were prosecuted for fraud, thereby gaining a criminal record, and over 100 booking clerks and station staff were dismissed.

In all, the budgeted fall in receipts due to the new zonal booking arrangements was £62 million; the actual fall

Princess Anne studying the controls of a tram as she opens the London Transport Museum in the former flower market of Covent Garden in March 1980. The Museum took over the London Transport Collection, which had been assembled at Syon Park from 1973 onwards, and has made many additions.   Ref. 192007–1

was only £46 million. About half of LT journeys were then made by bus pass or travelcard; by 1988–89, with one-day travelcards also available, the proportion had risen to 65 per cent. The cost of fare collection and, in particular, the delays at stops to one-man buses, were reduced.

The simplified fare structure resulting from zoning made much easier the spread of a new generation of more

sophisticated cash-fed ticket machines, a considerable advance on those originally tried out on the Victoria Line. Each station could now have its own computerised system of machines controlled from the ticket office, itself equipped with even more sophisticated ticket-issuing equipment (capable of issuing cards as well as tickets) and means of remotely controlling all the other ticket machines in the station. The whole was linked with a computer-controlled monitoring centre at Baker Street. Other equipment, installed on reversible gates also under booking office control, read each ticket. By 1989 nearly all stations on the system possessed ticket machines and Zone 1 stations had installed the new gates. 'The progressive introduction of the gates,' LRT reported, 'has led to a noticeable increase in revenue.'

Meanwhile, other changes were discernible on the Underground and bus services. The sanction, in 1981, of a ten-year rolling programme to improve 140 Underground stations was much welcomed at the time, although this activity, much of it cosmetic, may be seen in a rather different light in view of what we now know about the need to pay more attention to the station equipment and machinery.

The first dot matrix electronic indicator, telling passengers when the next two or three trains could be expected, was installed at St James's Park station in 1981 in place of the 70-year-old indicators which only showed the order of their arrival for the various routes. Dot matrix indicators soon became a familiar – and often a revealing – addition at other stations too.

While Underground passengers were told how long they would have to wait, those travelling by bus were provided with more shelters while waiting. In 1980 alone, 125 shelters were erected under the LT–Adshel joint venture scheme and a further 450 by LT which claimed then to provide 7,200 shelters at its 16,000 bus stops, together with about a thousand others owned by advertising companies or certain London boroughs. Two years later, with more added by LT–Adshel, the total had risen to 8,600.

The divisionalisation of the buses, modified in the light of experience, was

 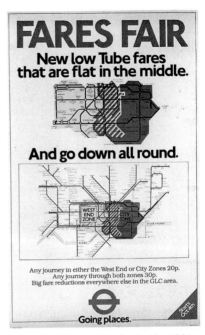

Fare zoning was introduced on bus routes within three miles of central London in May 1981 and was extended throughout London when the Fares Fair policy was launched in the following October. On the Underground, however, zoning was confined to the centre until May 1983, after which it covered the whole of the Underground network. Zoning had come to stay.
Refs. 24798 and 24799

followed by traffic studies, revised schedules and new routes, using smaller vehicles as required. In 1985–86 about 8 per cent of bus mileage was opened to competitive tender. Of 56 routes tendered, London Buses themselves won 26, National Bus subsidiaries 22, and private operators five. Full control of fares and services, however, was kept by LRT, as was all the fare revenue.

The only stretch of Underground railway opened during the decade was the link from Hatton Cross to Terminal 4 at Heathrow, and on to Heathrow Central, forming a loop. London Transport was also concerned with the Docklands Light Railway, built for most of its route high above ground level along disused railway bed and over an impressive new viaduct. It cost £77 million, which was provided partly by the Docklands Development Corporation with a special Department of Environment grant and partly by LRT, which was responsible for its operation. Author-

ised in 1982, the railway was officially inaugurated by the Queen on 30 July 1987 and opened for general traffic a few weeks later. The surface part of this railway had been built relatively cheaply; but it still had to be extended underground to the Bank and from the outset its capacity was too small.

In some respects the most valuable addition to London's railways during the 1980s was Thameslink. The reopening of Snow Hill tunnel in May 1988 allowed British Rail trains to cross through London between Bedford, Luton and St Albans in the north and Croydon, Gatwick Airport and Brighton in the south, thus restoring the direct connection which had been operated by steam trains earlier in the century. In 1990 the line was tunnelled under the foot of Ludgate Hill and the ugly railway bridge (see p. 33) that had for generations spoiled the view of St Paul's from Fleet Street was removed.

Fare zoning ended LT's loss of

(Right) Computerised ticket issuing and (below) reversible gates, both under booking office control in the restored Piccadilly Circus booking hall.

A welcome facelift for an ageing Underground platform. The emphasis in these refurbishments was on strong local themes. Ref. 23941–10

The experimental dot matrix indicator at St James's Park. Its 70-year-old predecessor can be seen in the background. Ref. C2182–11

traffic, especially on the Underground, on which the number of journeys increased from 498 million in 1982 to 769 million in 1986–87 (it reached 815 million by 1988–89). This extra burden, however, was unexpectedly imposed on a system by then growing distinctly elderly. Even the escalators in the central stations, built in the later

Between 1984 and 1987 an estimated 182 escalator fires on London's Underground were extinguished without causing injury. A disaster was waiting to happen – and it did. The scene on the surface above King's Cross Underground station on the evening of 18 November 1987.
The Press Association

1920s and 1930s, were nearing the end of their expected working lives. There were fires on some of them – subsequent evidence claimed 182 between 1983 and 1987 – caused by dropped matches or lighted cigarettes igniting decades of accumulated grease. Previous experience had shown that these fires, sometimes little more than smoulderings with no flame visible to passengers, soon died down when the grease had burned without setting the escalators themselves alight. The disastrous blaze at King's Cross on the early evening of 18 November 1987, nevertheless, when 31 lives were lost, demonstrated the enormity of the risks being taken.

The subsequent very long public

inquiry uncovered much else. The administrative reorganisation of a few years before may have achieved much at higher levels, but decentralisation left much to be desired lower down the managerial hierarchy. Staff, it was revealed, took greatly extended meal breaks when they should have been on duty, and platforms, and even the station itself, were left largely unmanned when the rush hour was over. If the staff had used the sprinkler and other equipment and the fire had been quenched before the 'flashover', the disaster would have been avoided. Attention would not have been drawn to LT's slowness in renewing the moving parts of its stations.

The programme of escalator and lift renewal was subsequently speeded up, but this made the traveller's task of getting through the stations even harder when traffic as a whole was continuing to grow. When the platform was reached, there were unduly long waits for trains, either because a train had been cancelled or because, running late,

it had to stop longer in each station to set down and pick up. The number of trains was certainly not increased to keep pace with the growth of traffic. With the consequent heavy overcrowding, travelling by Underground became more unpleasant and frustrating than it had ever been before in peacetime. And stringent new fire regulations resulted in unexpected, and often quite long, closing of stations and interruption of train services.

The bus services had been the subject of much enterprise in rerouteing, tendering and other efforts to grapple with growing traffic congestion on the roads – but, it seemed, to little effect. Waits at bus stops were long and unpredictable and when buses did arrive, they were apt to come in twos or threes. They did not redeem the bad name they had acquired from the 1960s onwards. It is significant that zoning, bus passes and travelcards did not cause bus traffic to pick up at the same rate as that on the Underground. The number of (much shorter) bus journeys, 1,040 million in 1982, reached only 1,244 million in 1988–89.

ON THE ROAD TO RECOVERY?

Londoners are paying a very high price for the long neglect of their public transport system. The time – and nervous energy – expended in struggling through Underground stations or standing in overcrowded trains, now increasingly at off-peak times as well as at rush hour, cannot be calculated; but London Transport estimates that traffic congestion costs bus passengers 55 million lost hours every year. This should be added to London Transport's own additional operating costs and lost revenue.

There are signs that public opinion is starting to stir, however. Politicians, ever mindful of the next election, are beginning to take notice. The extension of the Jubilee Line has been authorised, though via Parliament Square, not Charing Cross, and to Docklands, not Lewisham. Two new east–west lines across London are also under active consideration. The renovation of the existing Underground stations is slowly nearing completion. A start has been made on increasing the capacity of lines with new trains and signalling systems. It is conceivable that we may again be able to look forward to the kind of sustained, steady investment in the Underground that was a feature of the first 40 years of this century.

This brief historical survey suggests, however, that action to remove road congestion may be the main answer to London's problems. It was the buses which contributed the main share of LT's profits, and the whole organisation started to run into trouble when traffic from its road services had fallen to

half its peak level and went into operating deficit. The return of reliable bus services could restore its strength once again.

A growing body of opinion is coming to believe, on economic and environmental grounds, that drivers of cars and owners of commercial vehicles should be obliged to pay the cost which they inflict on other travellers when they clog the roads and prevent them

from being used for the purposes for which they were intended. (Those who block busy roads by parking, even to load and unload, are even greater offenders.) There is a strong case for, as a first step, paying almost all users of company cars in money and not in kind, thus treating them in the same way as everyone else. Company cars became more widely available in the 1970s, when the government's policy of in-

More shelters for those who waited.   Ref. 24808

(Above) Smaller buses on new routes. This Hoppa was photographed in Kensington in 1986.   Ref. 24212–11

(Right) The first tendered bus route through central London: the number 24 from Hampstead Heath to Pimlico, 1988.
Ref. 24804

come restraint caused employers to get round the law by providing them even for staff who did not need them for their jobs. The habit has flourished still more extensively in the 1980s. Employees in competing countries rarely enjoy such a privilege.

Methods have now been evolved, and tried out, whereby drivers can be charged for using roads at busy times, employing electronic signalling between roadside and vehicle. A specialist committee of the Chartered Institute of Transport, which represents all transport interests, has studied these methods and has explained in a lucid and detailed report, *Paying For Progress. A Report on Congestion and Road Use Charges* (March 1990), how electronic road pricing (ERP) would work. They have costed the various methods for the vehicle owner and the public authority, and they have estimated the total savings. 'The place where the greatest benefits from road pricing would accrue is London,' they believe. 'We recommend that the Government should now introduce a timetabled programme for the introduction of ERP in London in the mid-1990s. To delay any longer would be to sit back and accept billions of pounds worth of inefficiency in the national economy at the time when our competitiveness is coming under the greatest pressure.' 'Road pricing has arrived,' they conclude. 'The question is where it goes next.'

They suggest that prices would be fixed for each stretch of busy road and at various times of day at such levels that most drivers would be encouraged to go by another route, or at another time, or perhaps by public transport. For motorists entering the metropolis, large car

The trains on the Docklands Light Railway ran automatically, although each was manned by a train captain who could control it if necessary. The stations were generally unmanned, with tickets sold from machines. The initial City terminus, situated at high level overlooking Tower Hill, did not connect with the existing Underground when the railway was opened in 1987. Ref. 24804

parks would need to be provided on the outskirts at which they could switch to either bus or rail. Goods distributors, who now complain so bitterly about time and money lost in traffic, would either pay the road congestion charge if they thought it worth while or deliver goods at another time.

With traffic flowing again, and parking restrictions on main routes enforced by prompt removal of offending vehicles, the streets of London would look more like those of the 1930s, or even the early 1950s. There seems little hope that in the near future some major technical development will come to our aid comparable with the arrival of the electric motor or the petrol engine a century or so ago. But electronic devices can help us to clear the roads and so allow the buses, now fully developed, comfortable and efficient, to maintain fast, frequent and reliable services again, thus regaining passengers' confidence,

making profits for LT and easing crowding on the underground and suburban railways. Transponder devices which enable buses to change red traffic lights to green as they approach them are already being introduced. Electronic road pricing would take the process a stage farther by freeing the roads as well as the junctions.

The moment has arrived for this subject to be taken into the heart of the political arena. London has a great opportunity to leapfrog over the other great cities of the world and, by adopting road pricing, not only to take the lead in public transport once again but also to bring about dramatic reductions in atmospheric and noise pollution. Environmentalists, frustrated vehicle drivers and those still struggling to use public transport in its present state could form a powerful political lobby. It is up to us.

Index